DAVID BURNETT founded the Dovecote Press in 1974 in the small ha of Stanbridge near Wimborne to publish the first of three bestse illustrated books about Dorset, *A Dorset Camera 1855-1914*. Since he has been a central figure in local publishing, and the Dovecote Press has gone on to publish over 300 new titles, by authors as diverse as David Cecil, Jo Draper, John Fowles, James Lees-Milne and John Julius Norwich. Well over half have been about various aspects of Dorset's history and natural history. His own other books include *Dorset Camera 1914-1945*, *Dorset before the Camera*, *Dorset Shipwrecks*, *Dorset 1900-1999*, *The Twentieth Century in Photographs*, and *Dorset, The County in Colour*.

BARRY CUFF has been collecting books about Dorset since he was 15, later adding postcards after being given four Edwardian albums of local scenes and realising their value as a source of local history. What he describes as a 'fifty year addiction' now includes over 10,000 postcards of Dorset. He trained at the National Institute of Agricultural Botany, Cambridge, and his work as a seed analyst and crop inspector has taken him all over the country, from the Eden Project in Cornwall to running a winter bean breeding programme in Lincolnshire. He spent his childhood in Winterborne Whitechurch, and now lives in Sturminster Newton, where he is well known for his column in *Unity* on the ups and downs of his allotment.

Following pages
FARNHAM. There are many villages in Dorset that seem immune to change, and this view of Farnham is one. If the four girls in the foreground were still young today they could play in the small children's playground behind the railings that have replaced the wooden fence, but everything else would be familiar – as if frozen in time.
They might wonder why there is now a red telephone box near the railings, for like most rural boxes that has been made redundant by the invention of the mobile phone, and now serves as a village library.

THE DOVECOTE PRESS

LOST DORSET
The Villages & Countryside

DAVID BURNETT

The Barry Cuff Collection of Dorset Postcards 1880–1920

For Lily, Luca, Maisie and Sebbie. May they grow up to also love Dorset.

WEST KNIGHTON. The village fête in 1912.

First published in paperback in 2019 by The Dovecote Press Ltd
Stanbridge, Wimborne Minster, Dorset BH21 4JD

ISBN 978-0-9955462-8-8
Text © David Burnett
Illustrations © The Barry Cuff Collection

David Burnett and Barry Cuff have asserted their rights under the
Copyright, Designs and Patent Act 1988 to be identified as authors of this work

Typeset in Sabon and designed by The Dovecote Press Ltd
Printed and bound in India by Replika Press Pvt Ltd
All papers used by The Dovecote Press are natural, recyclable products
made from wood grown in sustainable, well-managed forests.

A CIP catalogue record for this book is available from the British Library

1 3 5 7 9 8 6 4 2

CONTENTS

INTRODUCTION

THE BEGINNING of a new decade seemed scant cause for celebration to most country folk in Dorset. 1879 had been one of the coldest and wettest years on record, bringing 'the summer that never was', a failed harvest and the death of large numbers of sheep from disease. Why should 1880 be any better? In Lydlinch, in the heart of the Blackmore Vale, Susan Basson, the National School's long-suffering mistress since its opening five years earlier, answered the question with an entry in the school log book by noting that the New Year was beginning with the same atrocious weather that had ended December, reducing attendance to forty, out of a possible seventy.

At Bloxworth, a day's journey away by pony and trap, and guided over the downs by small heaps of chalk a few yards apart, known as 'Dorsetshire milestones', Emily Hunt was nursing the newest addition to her family, the five-month-old Rose Elizabeth. Her husband Tom was a farmworker on the 3000 acre estate belonging to Colonel Jocelyn Pickard Cambridge, their home a tied cottage of wattle and daub (later to be demolished).

In September 1880 Tom, Emily and their children joined everyone else in Bloxworth to welcome the return of the Colonel's daughter from her honeymoon. The villagers had known Mary all her life. 'If you've got Miss Cambridge in there we're just going to pull her up!' they shouted, as the carriage bearing bride and groom entered the village. The men changed places with the horses, and amid much cheering and headed by a brass band from Lytchett Minster playing the 'British Grenadiers', bodily hauled the carriage to Bloxworth Lodge. In return, the Colonel promised a substantial lunch on the village green 'with their wives and sweethearts'. Despite the 'hearty cheers and numerous hurrahs' the Colonel must have looked out over his tenants with some concern, for like virtually every village in Dorset the population of Bloxworth's was in decline. (One casualty was Emily Hunt. Four years and three more children later, she left Tom a widower, dying in childbirth aged forty following

the birth of her eleventh child.)

Few of the postcards in *Lost Dorset* show evidence of the falling rural population, none its causes – of which death in childbirth was gradually becoming less frequent. 'In Weatherbury,' wrote Thomas Hardy (1840-1928) in *Far From the Madding Crowd* (1874), 'three or four score years were included in the mere present, and nothing less than a century set a mark on its face or tone. Five decades hardly modified the cut of a gaiter, the embroidery of a smock-frock, by the breath of a hair. Ten generations failed to alter the turn of a single phrase. In these Wessex nooks the busy outsider's ancient times are only old; his old times are still new; his present is futurity.'

If on the surface Dorset's villages and hamlets, its 'Wessex nooks', seemed impervious to external influences the truth is that the rural way of life chronicled by Hardy in his novels was undergoing radical and not always happy changes. For about twenty years from the middle of the 19th century Dorset farming enjoyed a 'Golden Age', bringing an improvement to the living standards of even the poorest. And there was ample need for it, as the housing and working conditions of the county's farm workers were amongst the worst in Britain.

Rachel Hayward, the wife of a Stourpaine labourer, was a witness to a Parliamentary Report of 1843. Her evidence described a family of eleven, three daughters and six sons, living in a two room cottage, in which everyone slept in one room. Her three eldest sons had started work aged nine, her daughters made Dorset buttons, adding to a wage packet that barely kept the family fed and clothed. They grew their own potatoes, which together with bread made with barley or second-class wheat formed much of their diet: it was estimated that in Dorset 10½ lbs of bread and 4½ lbs of potatoes were eaten per person per week. The only meat in her weekly budget was ½ lb of bacon. The bacon might have come from their own pig, whose keeping was common and enabled the enterprising housewife to vary a regime

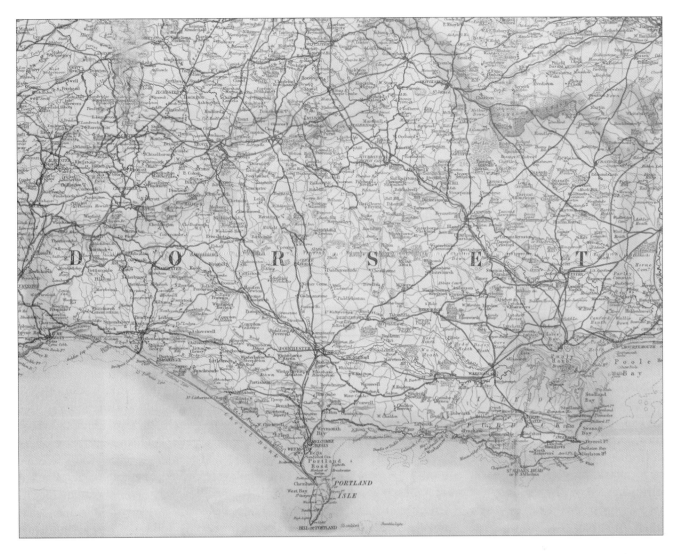

that was both monotonous and lacking in protein. But pigs make unhealthy neighbours.

That same Parliamentary Report cast a critical eye over those in Stourpaine: 'The matter constantly escaping from the pigsties, privies &c, is allowed to find its way between the cottages into the gutter in the street, so that the cottages are nearly surrounded by stream of filth.' Like elsewhere in rural Dorset, water came from wells or streams, there was no sanitation, the puddled chalk and stone-floored cottages were permanently damp, lit only by rush lights or candles.

A second report of 1867 found little had changed. 'The cottages in this county are more ruinous and contain worse accommodation than those in any other county I have visited,' wrote its commissioner. ' . . . such villages as Bere Regis, Fordington, Winfrith, Cranbourne, or Charminster . . . are a disgrace to the owners of the land, and contain many cottages unfit for human habitation.' The estate of Lord Rivers – Dorset largest landowner – was castigated as 'notorious for its bad cottages'. Of

the others, Fordington was owned by the Duchy of Cornwall, Cranborne by Lord Salisbury (later Prime Minister), and much of Charminster by Lord Alington and the Earl of Ilchester – collectively four of Dorset's wealthiest landowners.

If the day labourer living in an overcrowded tied cottage stood on the lowest economic rung, the one above belonged to the smallholder. Most owned their own cottages, either freehold or by copyhold for three lives, usually in villages not belonging to a single landowner or squire. The pig might have a cow or two for company, as well as bees and vegetables, giving their owner a measure of independence to work his own plot, however modest. 'There is no more comfortable or serene being than the cottager who is sure of his roof,' wrote Hardy, a statement echoed by his friend and fellow writer, the poet William Barnes.

> 'I got two vields, an' I don't care
> What squire mid have a bigger shëare.'

Barnes (1801-1886) was born in a small hamlet west of Sturminster Newton, and the poetry he wrote in his native Dorset dialect poetry harks back to the countryside of his childhood, to a way of life that clung on more tenaciously in the Blackmore Vale than elsewhere. Hardy described it as 'constructed on a smaller and more delicate scale.' Well-watered, a land of dairies and fields lined with hedgerow elms, Barnes's daughter thought 'the outer world had sent few echoes to disturb its serene and rustic quiet.' Even in the mid 19th century, she concluded, life in the Vale was that of the previous two centuries. But the clock does not stop. In 'The Common A-Took In', Barnes has two cottagers meet on the way to market and grumble about the loss of the common on which they – like everyone else – traditionally fattened their cattle and geese, cut gorse and briars for their ovens, and sent their children out in summer to gather 'A bag o'cow-dung vor to burn'.

The frugal self-sufficient smallholder celebrated by Barnes shared many of the characteristics of the craftsmen and tradesmen that kept the rural economy on its feet. Hazelbury Bryan is a few miles south of the poet's birthplace. In 1891 it had population of about 800. Of its twenty farms, the largest was 320 acres, the smallest nine. To ensure that ploughs were mended and horses shod, barns repaired, corn ground, the wheels kept on the waggon, the village could muster nine carpenters, four sawyers, four woodmen and hurdlemakers, four blacksmiths, four boot and shoe makers, two coopers, a wheelwright, a plumber, a saddler, a thatcher, a miller, and last, but surely not least, William Mullett, a 68-year-old blind mole catcher. Out of 417 women and girls, fifty worked as glovers, one as young as eight. To keep the village fed and clothed, there were four shopkeepers, three butchers, three bakers, three dressmakers, a fish dealer, three beerhouses, a pub, a draper and a seamstress. Charlotte Brownsea carried letters, Edwin Everett and an assistant mistress instructed their pupils in the 3Rs in the newly built school, the Anglican rector competed with the Welsh Primitive Methodist minister for the spiritual welfare of his flock, PC Henry Hoare kept the peace, and Joseph Lush hawked pots, pans and patent medicines around the outlying hamlets.

Many of these skills were passed down from father to son and could be found throughout Dorset. On the coast, netmaking replaced gloving as womens' work, just as button making did elsewhere in the Blackmore Vale, around Blandford and in the Isle of Purbeck. Purbeck's stone quarries provided the raw materials for a range of trades that had barely changed since medieval times.

What could not be so easily duplicated was Hazelbury Bryan's mixture of smallholdings and farms owned and worked by those who lived on them. A parliamentary report of 1873 paints a portrait of a county dominated by its landowning class. Of its 682,000 acres, 36% was owned by 10 families. Altogether there were 120 estates of more than 1,000 acres. Some villages, like Bloxworth, had belonged to the same family for 200 years, giving rise to the loyalty and affection that had welcomed Mary from her honeymoon. Others were owned by university colleges (Stour Provost) or boys public schools (Sydling St Nicolas, Piddletrenthide, Piddlehinton). The wealth generated by the Industrial Revolution and the expansion of the British Empire had added new money to old, further emphasizing the gulf between rich and poor. In her biography of Hardy, *The Time-Torn Man*, Claire Tomalin described Dorset as a county 'in which those who owned the land and those who worked it were hardly thought of as belonging to the same species.'

Rural Dorset was largely a hierarchy, at whose pinnacle sat its aristocratic landowners, followed by the gentry, parsons and middling squires. They were its magistrates, employers, owners of cottages, guardians of the Poor Law. The best built schools, and reading rooms, gave land for allotments. The worst were absentee, what Barnes called 'rich idlers'. Good or bad, in all but name they were the rulers of small kingdoms, and expected the deference that went with their status. However generous the allowance of coal, beer and faggots, there was always the fear of being turned out of a cottage if you crossed the squire or his agent.

The eccentric owner of Charborough Park, John Drax, went everywhere accompanied by his 'tiger', a small boy whose only task was to run alongside his master's gig and open and close gates. Mrs Sheridan of Frampton imperiously instructed Brunel to put his new railway in a 700 yard long tunnel so as not to spoil the view from her drawing room. Nathaniel Middleton, owner of much of Bradford Peverell, could carry out his duties as a magistrate certain that the smooth running of his house was in the safe hands of his eleven servants.

By chance, Bradford Peverell provides an example of an event that belongs to a rougher, even brutal, age. An entry in the school log book for 27 March 1863 reads: 'Some of the children went to Dorchester to see Mr Fooks and Mr Preedy hung.' Children aged six or seven. It was the last public hanging in Dorset, and was watched by a crowd of 5,000 – most of them women (two enterprising brothers erected a grandstand and charged for seats, which promptly collapsed beneath the weight).

I mention this because such an unlikely example of school truancy would have been unthinkable within twenty years. The rough and tumble gave way to the grinding task of earning a living through a period when rural Dorset was in crisis. Few of those facing the camera in the 350 postcards in this book are smiling. That might be the wariness with which country folk greeted an unfamiliar photographer asking them to pose for his camera. Even so, few of those gathered in village streets or going about their daily business appear contented with their lot. And with good reason. 1870 was farming's high-water mark. From then on came a decline that quickened pace as the century wore on, briefly slowed at the start of the 20th century, only to accelerate again in the years following the First World War.

As good a place as any to track the decline are the changing population figures between 1851 and 1901, of which these are random samples: Affpuddle 488 to 358, Cerne Abbas 1343 to 643, Hilton 761 to 502, Powerstock 1044 to 631, Whitchurch Canonicorum 1532 to 868. The appalling weather of 1879 was followed by a succession of failed harvests, but the seeds of the depression were already sown. Cattle plague in 1877 was followed by an unchecked outbreak of foot-and-mouth disease, which decimated herds. But farmers are resilient, used to changing fortunes. What they were totally unprepared for, and could do nothing about, was the untapped wealth of the American and Canadian prairies. Faster steamships and the growth of the railroad meant that grain could be shipped cheaply and quickly, leading to falling prices throughout Britain. Between 1871 and 1911 2,500,000 acres went out of cereal production as imports flooded in, counterbalanced by a corresponding increase in waste or pasture.

The final nail in farming's coffin was the arrival in London's docks in February 1880 of a Clyde-built steamer from Australia. The SS *Strathleven* had left Sydney just before Christmas 1879. Amongst its cargo, in a specially adapted refrigerated hold, were 34 tons of frozen mutton. Two years later it was followed by a vessel from New Zealand, the SS *Dunedin*, with 5,000 lamb and mutton carcasses on board. Within eight years New Zealand alone was annually exporting two million carcasses into British docks, as well as wool, cheese and butter.

These were blows that struck at the heart of what H.G. Wells called 'the unchanging rhythms of old-established agriculture'. The number of farmworkers fell by a third.

Businesses went bankrupt. Cottages were abandoned and pulled down (15 in Leigh within 20 years). Cerne Abbas's 14 pubs became three. Even the wealthiest landowners felt the pinch, as Lady Bracknell acutely observed in *The Importance of Being Earnest* (1894): 'Land has ceased to be either a profit or a pleasure. It gives one position and prevents one from keeping it up. That's all to be said about land.'

There were other changes afoot. Shipping advertisements in the *Dorset County Chronicle* offered the chance to begin a new life in the colonies, often lured by the promise of assisted passage for married labourers. 'Villages are left desolate that Canada, Australia and New Zealand may be populated,' wrote one vicar. Once reports reached the villages round Yetminster of the opportunities awaiting in Canada, rarely a month passed without would-be emigrants and their scanty bundles of possessions crowding the station platform.

A perceptive observer of the depression was Rider Haggard, author of *King Solomon's Mines*, whose travels round Britain to report on the state of farming for the *Daily Express* became a book, *Rural England*, published in 1903. Spotting yet another tumbledown cottage he wrote, 'How could a girl who had been in service be expected to live in a hovel when she married? Of course, the result was that she and her husband went away.' Many went to the towns, where the pay was better. Why stay in tiny Grimstone, described as 'squalid and dismal', when Bournemouth's bright gaslights and a job behind a shop counter beckoned?

One result as the century wore on was that the economic power of those who remained increased. Wages gradually rose. The labourer became more mobile, moving on from year to year. Old allegiances to the parish of your ancestors gave way to the search for better pay. Writing in Piddlehinton school log book on 5th April 1895 its mistress noted that 'This being the week the farmers change hands, many families have left the parish. During the last fortnight the school has lost 16 children.'

In 1883 Hardy tackled the subject in an essay for *Longman's Magazine* called 'The Dorsetshire Labourer.' As well as criticising the impact on a child's education of the annual Lady Day move from one farm to another by a worker and his family, he cast a quizzical eye over much else. His pleasure at the change of fortune of a local shepherd, whose cottage now boasted 'brass rods and carpeting to the staircase, and from the open door of which you hear a piano strumming within', was tempered by regret at the loss of much else.

He could not recall a single example of a farm labourer

still living on the farm on which he was born, linking it to a break in the accumulation of tradition and knowledge that bound a parish together, what we might call its DNA. Soon, he feared, no one would know the names of the neighbouring hills, streams and fields, the character and lives of those buried in the churchyard, the names of its fairies and ghosts, be able to recite its folk tales or sing its ballads, even search out the secret places where wild herbs could be gathered for medicine.

But there was much that could still be celebrated. All but Dorset's smallest hamlet were self-sufficient. Its inns, shops, school gate and blacksmith's forge provided a social heart where all could gather to gossip – of the coming harvest, a birth, a young couple whose courtship was no longer a secret. The seasonal cycles of farming and the Christian church created a calendar of holidays that punctuated the year and all looked forward to. In the winter a fiddler would tune up in the school room, and there would be a sing-song or dancing. The summer brought feast and fair days. There would be stalls, swing boats and races. Autumn meant the Harvest Supper, with trestles the length of the barn and a barrel or two of cider. Christmas welcomed the annual appearance of the mummers and their attendant hobby horse.

On May Day in Shillingstone, sprigs of oak with gold tinsel stuck on the leaves were distributed round the village. Bunting decorated the cottages. There was a fair round the stump of the stone cross. After dancing to a local band, and a detour to the Old Ox Inn for liquid refreshment, the entire population marched to the 118 feet high maypole, where to the beating of drums and waving of banners the garlands were duly hung and everyone joined hands and careered wildly round the maypole until darkness fell. Similar celebrations took place in every village.

But it is hard not to think of those 'lads and their maidens' linking arms round the maypole and remember that I am writing this in 2018, a hundred years since the end of the First World War. Many of those young men would join the Dorsetshire Regiment or Yeomanry, serving in India, the Middle East and the Western Front. For others it was the Royal Navy, or the fledgling Royal Air Force. All too many would not return, leaving their 'maidens' widows. *Lost Dorset* is a portrait of a way of life that existed when they left, but like a slow-fading photograph was already disappearing when they finally came home.

Though he was safely in his grave long before the war ended, William Barnes wrote their epitaph – and an elegy to the world they had left behind:

> 'An 'oft do come a saddened hour
> When there must goo away
> One well-beloved to our heart's core
> Vor long, perhaps voy aye:
>
> An' oh! it is a touchen thing
> The loven heart must rue,
> To hear behind his last farewell
> The geäte a-vallèn to.'

DELIVERING THE POST

HOLME. A postman on Holme Lane, near Wareham, in about
1910. By then the lane was a leafy backwater, but until the
opening of the turnpike (the present A352) it had been the
main route between Wareham and Wool.

This book would not exist but for the decision in 1870 by the General Post Office to introduce a halfpenny stamp for postcards. Initially, they were pre-stamped, the address going on one side, the writing on the other. In 1894 the GPO changed tack, allowing an image on one side, writing and address on the other. Britain's High Street photographers wasted no time in venturing out into the countryside in search of suitable subjects for picture postcards. Within 20 years not far short of a billion were being pushed through letterboxes or handed to a postman on his round.

The post office was once as much a part of rural life as its pub or church. It was a social hub, often doubling as the village shop. Services introduced towards the end of the 19th century, and which we now take for granted, changed the lives of even the humblest citizen. By 1900 you could send a parcel as well as a letter or postcard, buy a postal order, pay into a savings fund, contribute to an annuity or life insurance. Many were telegraph offices, allowing the sending of telegrams. Even the smallest hamlet acquired a bright red wall letter-box, of which only a handful stamped 'VR' for Queen Victoria survive.

With 225,000 employees, many of them women, the General Post Office formed the largest workforce in Britain and the daily appearance of the postman was the most familiar manifestation of the state in ordinary lives. A job with the GPO was much sought after, not least because it offered a range of benefits unheard of elsewhere – including free medical facilities, paid holidays, a pension scheme, and the possibility of promotion. There was a uniform, on which good conduct stripes for exemplary service were worn until 1914. Pay was based on length of service and job category. There was a complex pecking order of grades and ranks, of which the rural postman shown pushing his bike along Holme Lane on the previous page was close to the bottom.

The growth of the postal system marched hand in hand with that of the railway network. Once the post had reached a central sorting office (Dorchester, Poole etc), it was taken by horse and trap to the surrounding villages first thing in the morning, or by train if it boasted a station, then sorted into the various rounds by a self-employed sub-postmaster or mistress who received scaled payments for the work and a fee for supervising salaried postmen, who carried the post in 'pouches' for delivery within their parish. All rounds were on foot, called the 'Walk'. Bloxworth's postman, Frank Squire, is reckoned to have walked 165,000 miles during his 42 years of service.

Many rounds were so long that tin huts were provided, complete with bunk and a coal stove, so that the postman could have a rest once he had completed his deliveries. A nap and cup of tea later, he retraced his route, clearing his boxes as he walked. Not all completed their round. In 1897 poor Joseph Rogers of Cerne Abbas was overbalanced by the weight of his mailbag and accidentally fell into a well, the waterlogged cause of his death still slung round his shoulders when he was found.

In 1900 bicycles were issued: a cycling postman covered up to 26 miles a day. Vans and motorbikes with sidecars didn't make an appearance on country lanes until after the First World War. The first post office was often just a cubby hole in a cottage, as at Melbury Abbas where in 1875 Reginald Spinney combined five occupations – postmaster, blacksmith, shopkeeper, music teacher and dentist (for the last of which he made his own tools).

The creation of a national postal service enabled families and loved ones to keep in touch for the first time in their lives. The halfpenny card was the modern equivalent of a text message. Many were written in the afternoon for delivery the following morning, occasionally to someone in the same village. Sadly, few of those sent and included in *Lost Dorset* say much of any note. Most were written on holiday and include the usual English preoccupation with the weather. Some betray a struggle with forming letters. Others merely record safely reaching Dorset or an intended departure date.

One service both writer and recipient could guarantee was the prompt arrival of their postcards. There were up to three collections a day, as well as a Sunday Walk, which householders could opt out of for religious reasons. Kelly's *Directories* list the precise details for every village in the county. Puddletown's entry for 1895 is typical. Letters were received by mail cart from Dorchester; delivered at 7 a.m. and 2 p.m., and dispatched at 10 a.m. and 7.15 p.m.. And this took place seven days a week, whatever the weather.

BOCKHAMPTON. Mr Burgess, the postman, stands outside the post office/village shop in 1912. Burgess was the husband of the then headmistress of the village school, which lay behind the wall on the left and whose most celebrated pupil was Thomas Hardy, who went there aged eight in 1848, the year after it opened. The post office took longer to arrive, opening in 1881 and closing in 1970. For all 90 years it was run first by Mary Bartlett, followed by her daughter Alice.

Alice rarely went to bed before midnight; eating breakfast at dinner time, dinner at tea, and tea at supper – which made the shop's opening hours unpredictable. Both school and shop are now private houses, though the entrance porch to the school with the bell hanging above it has been preserved. A modern photograph taken on the same spot would be virtually identical: only the hedge and trees now growing above the wall would be unfamiliar to the children in the lane.

BUCKLAND NEWTON. Though the building is no longer a post office, both it and the adjoining wheelwright's cottage remain unchanged. Today a part time postal service operates out of the Village Hall three mornings a week. Note the motorbike parked outside. The photograph dates to shortly before the First World War, when George Mitchell was the postmaster and Hiram Russell the wheelwright. The post was delivered from Dorchester by mail cart at 6.25 a.m.

Above: CHESELBOURNE. The woman standing in the doorway is probably the wife of John Riggs, who combined running the post office with his work as village wheelwright and blacksmith. The thatched extension was listed as a 'barton' in the 1850 census, and at some point the building was home to the village carrier, hence 'Carriers', its name today. The cottage beyond has since been demolished.

Below: CHICKERELL. The post office, West Street, just before the First World War. Beyond it is the Methodist Chapel of 1865, which still has regular services. Chickerell was a stronghold of NonConformity, once supporting Wesleyan, Congregationalist and Baptist chapels, as well as the Methodists and Plymouth Brethren. Oddly, for NonConformity went hand in hand with the Temperance Movement, it also supported six beer retailers and a pub.

Post Office, Chickerell.

CHIDEOCK. William and Kate Foss in the doorway of their shop, Sweets Cottage, in the summer of 1911. The man holding the baby boy was a Mr Marshall, on holiday and staying in the cottage. Foss's was a 'Cycle Agent' and tobacconist, and the first shop in the village to sell paraffin and petrol. It went on to become a garage and the post office, a role it still fills today. The Foss's daughter Kathleen Symes was postmistress until 1995 and it is still run by the family. Note the postmen with their bicycles, and the 'good conduct' stripe worn on the jacket of the one on the left.

CHURCH KNOWLE. The post office and village shop in about 1900. This building burnt down and was never rebuilt. Emily Manuel was then the postmistress, beginning a link with the family that survived the move to a cottage opposite the Reading Room and lasted for over a century, until the retirement of Mary Wrixon in about 2003.

CREECH. The post and telegraph office in about 1903, when Mrs Edith Talbot was the sub-postmistress. Set back near Creech Grange down a short track off the lane between Stoborough and Steeple, this most unlikely post office and village shop was built by the Bond family for their estate tenants. The neatly laid hedge has gone, but the gate remains – as does the square Georgian-style house, with an 'ER' letterbox set into one wall.

Post Office, Durweston.

Post Office, East Chaldon.

Opposite page top: DURWESTON. A view down Water Lane in about 1895, when George Hayward was the village shopkeeper, postmaster and carpenter. The post office later moved to opposite the church, but the shop remained there until it finally closed.

Opposite page bottom: EAST CHALDON. The post office and shop stood to one side of the triangular village green, not far from the Sailor's Return inn. Much of the ditch in the foreground has been replaced by a neat sloping lawn, and the post office is now a private house. The old village pump is another survivor.

Above: EVERSHOT. An obviously posed photograph of a woman posting a letter. In 1895 Evershot's population was 371 and John Pouncy was the postmaster. Letters arrived from Dorchester at 6.40 a.m. and 1 p.m. and were despatched at 10.30 a.m. and 6.50 in the evening – seven days a week and in winter. The building is now a private house, though Evershot retains a post office and village shop. Evershot's links with the Earls of Ilchester and the Melbury Estate gave it a wider infrastructure than many much larger villages. It had a solicitor, medical officer, schoolmaster, constable, wood turner, boot and shoe maker, general stores, beer seller, two inns, builder and undertaker, dressmaker, shopkeeper, baker, butcher, blacksmith, tailor, haulier, and an agent for agricultural implements.

Above: LEIGH. Outside Denbury House, then the post office, in about 1905. The same family served as postmaster and postmistress for over 80 years, initially Mr and Mrs Sargeant, and from 1951 their daughter Gwen Gosney, who remained postmistress until well into the 1980s. Today the post office is at Bridge Garage. Notice the baker's hand cart and the army recruiting poster to the right of the door. The post was delivered to the village every morning by horse and trap from Sherborne. The village blacksmith was responsible for their maintenance, in winter either knocking frost nails into the horse's hooves or scraping grooves into them to prevent slipping on icy lanes.

Below: LEIGH, TOTNELL. Mr Sargeant, the postman, outside Totnell Cottage on Totnell Hill, possibly when it was occupied by a Miss Lane. The cottage remains little changed.

LULWORTH CAMP P.O. 1911

LULWORTH. Lulworth Camp post office in 1911. The arrival of the army on Purbeck dates to 1896 when the War Department bought 100 acres of heathland near Bovington as a rifle range. More land was gradually acquired for the thousands of soldiers temporarily housed under canvas for musketry training. By 1914 huts stood alongside the tents, and there were camps at Lulworth, Bovington and Worgret near Wareham. Of the three, Lulworth was the most basic, with tents being blown away by the south-westerly gales sweeping up Bindon Valley. In 1916 it became the home of the Tank Gunnery School, a role it still performs, and whose ranges include Tyneham and a large stretch of coastal land.

MELCOMBE BINGHAM. The post office and village shop in about 1895, when Mrs Caroline Chaldecott was the sub-postmistress. This lovely flint and brick cottage, with its hood moulded doorway, served as the money order and telegraph office for many of the surrounding villages, as well as an annuity and insurance office. Mrs Chaldecott's husband, James, ran the shop and was also a blacksmith. The cottage still stands, its flink and brick hidden behind render.

TARRANT MONKTON. At some point in the 1880s the village baker and shopkeeper Albert Goulding became its sub-postmaster as well, opening a postal counter in his cottage near the Langton Arms. Both shop and post office moved later, including for a brief period into the Langton Arms. The cottage has since been converted into two dwellings.

elcombe Bingham Post Office.

TYNEHAM. Post Office Row. The first cottage on the left was the post office and shop. Like the manor house and virtually the entire village, the row is now a roofless overgrown ruin. This is the first of three Tyneham photographs in the book, the village and 3,000 acre Purbeck estate owned by the Bond family since the end of the 17th century. In 1943 the entire estate was requisitioned for tank training in the build up to D-Day and the village was evacuated, falling victim to a broken Government promise that it would be returned to its rightful owners after the war. The land is still occupied by the Ministry of Defence and used for live firing and tank training.

WINTERBORNE WHITECHURCH. The Post Office and Telegraph Office in about 1907. William Snook, the postmaster, is on the left. Next to him is Miss Jenkins who worked behind the counter. The mail was brought to Whitechurch from Blandford by horse and van twice daily at 6.15 am and 1.30 pm. From here it was sorted and delivered to Winterborne Kingston, Milton Abbas and Milborne St Andrew, either by bicycle or pony and trap. Hence the other five postmen in the photograph.

CHILDHOOD & SCHOOLS

MORETON. Titled 'The Mudlarks', the card shows a group of children playing beside the
bridge over the River Frome, with the ford visible in the background. The card was sent to
the daughter of the Milborne St Andrew policeman; 'here is a little dirty lot for you down
at the long bridge playing with mud.'

Childhood in Victorian rural Dorset was precarious and uncertain. Sixteen percent did not live to celebrate their ninth birthday. Disease swept through entire communities, encouraged by damp, diet and overcrowding. The first entry in Enmore Green's school log book is for November 1862: 'School small on account of fever and chicken pox prevailing throughout the parish.' Eight years later, in Puddletown, an epidemic of scarlet fever killed nine children.

There was no knowledge of birth control, marriage often taking place only when the prospective bride became pregnant. Families tended to be large. In 1911, the long-suffering wives of a Tincleton carter, William Cheffey, and his farm labourer brother George had 16 children between them, the youngest a fortnight old.

Until the passing of the 1870 Education Act, rural education in Dorset for the 'poor' was limited to dame schools (often a widow), Church of England National schools, and those built and maintained by a wealthy landowner. In the wake of the 1870 act attendance was made compulsory between the ages of five and ten, and part-time attendance to fourteen. The weekly fee (2d for the first child, 1d for the others) was gradually abolished.

Throughout the county new elementary Board Schools sprung up, paid for by local government and run by an elected School Board. The rules for Bloxworth's (1873) are typical: the building was to be 'used for the education of children and adults, or children only of the labouring, manufacturing and other poorer classes of the Parish of Bloxworth, and for no other purpose.' They were usually built in a single storey red brick Victorian style that makes them easily recognisable. Some had an adjoining schoolhouse for the master or mistress. Few had more than one school room. At Spetisbury the children drank from a bucket drawn from a well. Ashmore School had no clock, ending lessons when the light fell through a window on a certain mark. At Lytchett Matravers the pupils were taught to write the alphabet in trays of sand. Although a handful are still primary schools today, most have closed and either been demolished or given a new lease of life as village halls.

Legislation was one thing, rural realities quite another. A succession of parliamentary reports record the widespread use of rural child labour and its impact on health. Working children were an important source of income, providing extra hands in the field. One report describes boys as young as seven working from 5 am to 7 pm to help with the ploughing and carting. Girls scared birds, picked stones, weeded crops. Dorset's school log books, which legally had to be kept by the schoolmaster or mistress, regularly list absences by both girls and boys for potato planting, haymaking, and harvest. The beginning of the autumn term was often delayed by a late harvest.

As virtually every child walked to school, some two or three miles each way, few weeks passed without such entries as 'All classes thin owing to a wet morning'. Snow or bad weather closed a school completely. One winter at Gussage All Saints the childrens' fingers became so numb with cold they couldn't hold their slates. Punishment varied, and was occasionally brutal. In Sixpenny Handley a boy was placed across a desk and thrashed for leaving through the window not the door.

Rural education largely consisted of the three Rs, and there were high levels of illiteracy. When Rhyme Intrinseca school opened in 1875 its teacher, Emily Hoare, noted that her 12 pupils were 'particularly backward' and that one 12-year-old boy did not know his letters. Even at the end of the century the syllabus still reflected the narrow range of occupations that lay ahead for most country children – domestic service for the girls and farm labouring for the boys. Basic agriculture was taught, as were needlework and laundry work. At Trent, where until the 1870s the pupils stood throughout their lessons, the curriculum expanded to include reading, writing, arithmetic, singing, history and geography.

As in many schools, the rector was a regular visitor, usually to instruct from the Bible or put on a magic lantern show. The lady of the manor often acted as Lady Bountiful, treating the children to an annual tea or supplying material for making up into shirts and petticoats. At Cerne Abbas, the then Lady Digby gave a medal and a new pair of boots to the prize-winners for attendance.

The quality of the teaching depended on the schoolmaster or mistress, assisted in the infants class by a pupil-teacher, usually a girl. Salaries were small (£65 for the head teacher), but teaching offered an escape from domestic service. Both Hardy's sisters trained as teachers, as did Fancy Day, the heroine of *Under the Greenwood Tree* (1872).

But there were compensations. The log books list day's off for Empire Day (May 24 and intended to 'remind children what it meant to be sons and daughters of such a glorious Empire'), local fairs and fêtes, royal weddings and birthdays. There were Sunday School outings and May Day celebrations. Wool's school outing of 1894 describes a convoy of farm waggons with flags flying and 'full of bright shining faces' setting out for Arish Mell. Games included marbles, hopscotch, conkers and bowling a hoop. There were no motorcars or lorries to worry about. It was a simple uncomplicated childhood, free of today's stresses and anxieties, with field and hedgerow outside the door.

ALDERHOLT. Children lined up outside the village school in 1913, when a Charles Bracher was master. The school opened in 1847 and was enlarged the year before this photograph was taken as the heathland village had grown substantially. The postcard was sent to a South Kensington address with a note saying 'one for your album' and naming the two children marked with a x on the front of the card. The Daggons Road building still stands, and is now Kings Wood Day Nursery.

The card below was sent by a young assistant teacher called Lily lodging near the school. The back reads, 'This will show you the house where I am staying. I have marked my room. Another of the teachers lodges in the second of the brick houses, so we are often together. Love from Lily.' Both houses remain unchanged, though a modern view would include the War Memorial bearing the 18 names of the villagers who died during the First World War.

Model Village, Canford, Wimborne.

CANFORD MAGNA. The cottages either side of the lane were the work of Lady Charlotte Guest, the philanthropic wife of the Welsh ironmaster Sir John Guest, who had bought the Canford Estate in the mid 19th century, adding to the house (now Canford School) and doing much to improve conditions for those living on the estate. The two surviving blocks of terraced cottages were built between 1870 and 1872, complete with gables, ornamental chimneys and large rear gardens, for a fixed rent of a shilling a week.

The School, Childe Okeford.

Ciffey Childe Okeford.

CHILD OKEFORD. Outside the school shortly before the First World War. The 1846 school was much enlarged in 1874 and by the time this photograph was taken had 200 pupils. Here are the Infants Class, with their mistress Miss E.M. Trim. It has since closed and is now a private house.

AN EARLY MORNING DIP.

DANCING LEDGE. 'An Early Morning Dip'. The pool was blasted out of the cliff quarry-shelf by Thomas Pellat, the first headmaster of Durnford House, described as a 'traditionally brutal' boys prep school in Langton Matravers. One victim of Pellat's morning ritual of 'strip and swim' was Ian Fleming, the author of the James Bond novels, for whom the school 'epitomised the strange British faith in bad food, plenty of Latin and beatings from an early age.' The school was taken over as part of the coastal radar network during the Second World War and its pupils transferred to another school, the Old Malthouse, which closed in 2007.

ENMORE GREEN. A rare view of the interior of a classroom. Although Enmore Green is on the northern edge of Shaftesbury, it lies in the parish of Motcombe and was still very rural in the late 19th century. The school opened in 1862, amalgamating with St James School, Shaftesbury, a century later, and is now the flourishing Abbey Church of England Voluntary Aided School at the foot of Gold Hill. Note the oil lamp, and sign on the wall saying 'Our motto, Be Punctual'. The school log books, 1862 – 1885, are held in the Dorset History Centre and reveal much about the difficulties faced by a young schoolmistress trying to educate the children in her care.

FARNHAM. Just out of view on the right is the small village school, which opened in 1837 and is now a private house. The 18th century cottages with their gable ends to the lane were all built by General Pitt-Rivers, the pioneering 19th century archaeologist, and were part of the Pitt Rivers Estate.

FARNHAM.

Above: FERNDOWN. May Day in about 1910. The village grew up on the edge of the heath and was originally part of Hampreston parish. Its few scattered cottages mostly belonged to nurserymen or smallholders, but by the date of this photograph had a population of over 1,000 and had acquired shops, a chapel and church as well as the elementary school (built 1901 for 60 children). May Day customs were revived in the latter part of the 19th century by the church and school authorities, who purged them of their former boisterousness.

FONTMELL MAGNA. The school's 140 children doing their daily exercises for the benefit of the photographer in the school yard in 1913, with Gable Cottage on the right. The 1902 Education Act added regular physical education to the curriculum. Until 1926 virtually the entire village was owned by the banking Glyn family, and it was they who paid for the building of the West Street school in 1864, as well as houses for both a master and matron. The school is now St Andrew's Church of England Primary School and has about 180 pupils.

HAMPRESTON. Outside the school in about 1910 when it had 170 pupils. The school was paid for by Lady Charlotte Guest and opened in 1874. It served a large area, including Little Canford, Longham, Little Moors and, until its own school opened in 1914, Ferndown as well – with virtually all the children making the journey on foot. Its first five teachers were a 'Miss', whose duties included making sure that all the girls could sew before they left the infants. The Church of England First School is still open with about 75 pupils. Its history and entries from its Victorian and early 20th century logbooks have been posted on its website.

HILTON. 'This is the school where I stay,' wrote Mabel on this card, adding love and a line of kisses to 'My dear Wilfy'. The brick and flint school was opened in 1863 for 120 children and paid for by the Hambro family of Milton Abbey, who also bore the cost of the adjoining house for the mistress. Note the sturdy Dorset gate. The school closed in 1982 and is now privately owned.

HOLT. Children playing on the Green in about 1900. The adjoining school was built in 1840 on land belonging to the Bankes Estate, who owned the village and surrounding farms until an auction in 1919. The school closed in 1973 and is now the village hall. Until 1894 and the creation of Dorset County Council Holt was in the parish of Wimborne, and remains one of only a handful of villages in Dorset to retain a Green.

HOLT, GAUNTS COMMON. Boys gardening outside the National School in about 1910. The school opened in 1856 and was partly paid for and maintained by Sir Richard Glyn, on whose Gaunts Estate it stood. As St James' Church of England VC First School it still flourishes today, and in the original building.

LEIGH. The village cross, with its medieval base and shaft and 19th century cross. Cross House, the house in the background on the lane to Chetnole, is little changed: remarkably, the railings have survived. Just outside the photograph, on the left, is the old village school, now converted into two cottages. This card was posted to Canada in January 1908, probably to someone who had recently emigrated, for on the back it reads 'that is Mrs Loveless in the doorway. Gloomy, foggy weather.' – sentiments that can only have reinforced the recipient's reasons for leaving Dorset.

LITTON CHENEY. Children in Chalk Pit Lane in about 1900. The first cottage on the right was also the post office. When the row was modernised in 1909 (and given a stone plaque saying 'Graves Cottages) the thatch was replaced with tiles, despite Abbotsbury's reed beds being only a few miles away.

Litton Cheney.

Lydlinch School. Dorset.

LYDLINCH. Children outside the National School in the early 1920s. The school opened in 1874 and could accommodate 70 children. Entries from the log books until 1920 have been transcribed by Caryl Parsons and are available on the website – hence this entry by the schoolmistress from September 1899: 'I find the boys very unruly and disobedient. This afternoon I had occasion to punish William and Frank Parsons. They succeeded in taking the cane out of my hand, and breaking it to pieces, accompanying the action with some low remarks. I felt myself justified in turning them out of the school, which I accordingly did.' The small boy third from the right on the front row was William Frizzle, whose wife Mary is now in her nineties and still living in Lydlinch. The school is now a private house.

MARNHULL. Children outside St Mary's Catholic School at the corner of Old Mill Lane and Great Down Lane, which opened in 1897 on the edge of the village and was paid for by a French priest, Father Alexander Dodard, also the unlikely owner of Marnhull's first motorcar. Catholicism in Marnhull dates back to the purchase of Nash Court by the Hussey family in 1651 and it was the Husseys who in 1846 provided land near the end of the lane for the first Catholic school and a teacher's house for its six pupils. The School moved again to the site of a former convent in 1953 and the two buildings in the photograph are now private houses. St Mary's continues to flourish, and is now the oldest Catholic primary school in the West Country.

MILBORNE ST ANDREW. The inmates and staff of Dorset County Industrial School for Boys in about 1900. I say 'inmates' rather than 'pupils' because in all but name the school was a a Borstal for young offenders. It was originally a reformatory founded in 1856 by the philanthropist John Clavell Mansel (later Mansel-Pleydell) of nearby Whatcombe for boys under 16 sentenced to detention for less than five years. The boys learnt various trades, including horticulture, tailoring, carpentry and poultry-keeping. There were two fully rigged masts in the grounds for those who hoped to go to sea, and a band offered the chance to become a military bandsmen. It was a tough regime: boys who wet their beds had their mattresses strapped to their backs. In 1919 the *Poole & Dorset Herald* included an article stating that some of the boys are 'skin and bone' and were being 'sent out to work for farmers on a breakfast of bread, milk and water and the poor lads are veritable slaves of the land'. Perhaps unsurprisingly it closed the following year and after various changes of fortune (during the Second World War it became a POW Camp) it is now run as an independent Christian charity called Longmead Community Farm.

Left: MILTON ABBAS. The school opened in 1840 and was paid for by the Hambro family, who had bought the Abbey and Estate in 1852. As late as the 1930s there were two schoolrooms, one for infants, the other for 7 to 15 year-olds. There were no washbasins and the outside toilets consisted of wooden seats over buckets. The building on the left was the master's house. The school closed in 2002 and has since been converted into a private house.

Centre: MORETON. The village school opened in 1860 and is now the popular Moreton Tearooms, a regular winner of Taste of the West Awards. The writer of the card, a teacher at the school, didn't much care for Moreton, describing it as 'down in a hole.'

Below: OWERMOIGNE. Children gathered on the Moreton road near the forge in about 1890. Just visible on the right is the village 'pile', a brick platform where water could be drawn from a well. The low thatched barn and thatched cottage in the background no longer stand and this view is completely unrecognisable today.

The School, Moreton.   G. Purchass, Moreton.

Above: PIDDLETRENTHIDE. Children beside the River Piddle at Lover's Bridge in about 1900.

Below: PORTESHAM. 'Put us on a postcard, Sir!' Note the spelling of 'Portisham', which was supposedly changed to avoid confusion with Portsmouth when the railway arrived in 1885. In this 1905 view of Front Street a Dame School stood on the right (now Chestnut Cottage). It was one of four in the village, allowing a mid-19th Parliamentary Select Committee to conclude that Portesham's 'poorer classes have sufficient means of education.' The shop on the right was a baker, and the large building on the right in the background is Trafalgar House, where a Mr Bartlett kept a few cows and pigs.

RHODEHORN

SOUTH PERROTT

Above: RHODE BARTON. Primroses cover a hillside at Rhode Horn north of Lyme Regis on the county boundary with Devon. The children sold the flowers in Lyme Regis and Charmouth.

Left: RYME INTRINSECA. The schoolmistress and her assistant with some of their pupils outside the little village school with its single room. The school was founded by John Blennerhassett, the vicar for 60 years, opening in 1875 with 41 children, though average attendance was often half that. It seems to have been badly run and given little equipment or books. Transcribed extracts from the school log book include successive mistresses reports, as this by Mary Lucas in May 1883: 'Children not allowed their usual recreation this week as punishment, not being able to do as they were told. Gave them lesson on "Disobedience" instead. They have promised to behave better for the future. Taught Infant's school song "The Little Sweep" and older children "The Harvest Field". Needlework very bad and dirty, have asked the Treasurer for a bowl, towels and soap for the children to wash their hands, and material for to learn to work, have supplied it myself since I came. Have asked for more slates, only 7 fit for use, for another easel and B.Board, and for pegs in the Porch for children's clothes, and more copy books and exercise books.' The school is now a private house.

Left: SOUTH PERROTT. Church Hill in about 1900. The gates at the top lead into the churchyard. The first cottage on the left was built in the late 18th century as a tied cottage to the adjacent farm. The building just visible behind the tree on the right has since been demolished and replaced. This is probably near the old village well.

Above: STRATTON. Children on an old wooden bridge over the River Frome in the early 20th century.

Below: TOLPUDDLE. The Cross and Martyrs Tree in about 1890. It was here in 1834 that six farm labourers, the Tolpuddle Martyrs, used to meet under the sycamore on the left, a place celebrated as the birthplace of the Trades Union Movement. The tree still stands. In 2002 it was designated one of the 50 most historic trees in Britain, and has recently been pruned and pollarded to encourage new growth.

Above: WEST STAFFORD. The Forge and Davine are almost exactly opposite the old school house in the middle of the village, and were initially three cottages rented from the Floyer Estate by the Greening family, the village's first blacksmiths.

Below: WINTERBORNE WHITECHURCH. The headmaster Thomas Jones lived in a large house attached to the school and taught the seniors. Miss Dora Shave, shown here on the left, taught the young ones. There were two playgrounds, one for the boys and the other for the girls.

VILLAGE LIFE

ASHMORE. Eden Cottage on the left is the larger of two cottages and a washhouse that once stood at the bottom of Green Lane. Thanks to George Taylor, who until recently has lived all his life in Ashmore, we know that Henry Davidge, who was a lay preacher at the Mission Hall near the top of the lane, lived in Eden Cottage, and Florence Rideout lived in the one on the right. The washhouse still stands, rebuilt as a single storey house, whilst the two cottages were demolished in 1960.

No two dorset villages are the same. Hardy classified them as of three types: 'the village cared for by its lord, the village cared for by itself, and the village uncared for either by itself or by its lord.' This book provides samples of each. Yet the life lived in them was similar, only the means of earning a wage varying. Those on the coast were largely reliant on fishing and netmaking. Brickworks and building trades supported those closest to the towns, especially in the south-east where Bournemouth was rapidly expanding across once empty heath. Purbeck's few villages had long lived off stone quarrying, more recently helped by the digging of clay. Elsewhere, be it well-wooded Cranborne Chase or the rolling central downland, the fertile valley of the Frome or the Blackmore and Marshwood vales, it was agriculture and the skills that oiled farmings' wheels that shaped the character of rural Dorset.

Apart from the parish church, the largest buildings in the village were usually the manor house, manor farm, or rectory. The words 'manor house' suggest a resident squire, which was not always the case. Some were divided into tenements, others were working farms. A few were rented out by absentee landlords, often to retired military officers or families with private means – something which became increasingly common as land values and the income from farming fell. But as the postcards make clear, *Lost Dorset* is not about the wealthy – principally because photographs of them are all too often formal portraits or family groups. The men, women and children in this book are what Hardy called 'workfolk', ordinary village people going about their daily business.

Their homes were simple. In *Highways and Byways in Dorset* Frederick Treves described the Dorset cottage as 'apt to be low, so low that it would be simpler to alight from the bedroom windows than to descend the ladder-like stairs.' The old Dorset saying that you courted ill-luck by living in a house more than one room wide sounds like a convenient excuse for hard-nosed reality. As late as the 1890s many cottages comprised a 12 ft x 12 ft living room with a back kitchen or scullery. Upstairs were two bedrooms, one large, one small, often reached by a ladder. A Parliamentary Report into housing in Cerne Abbas noted that the rooms were only six feet high, the windows not made to be opened, with a single privy serving five or six cottages. Privies in the downland villages were known locally as 'sit-still's', the bucket being emptied weekly into a hole dug in the garden (in the case of Turnworth until 1956). In a memoir of life in Dewlish, Bernard Marsh recalled the privy as being at the bottom of the garden with a vault under, which was cleared once a year.

Bernard also remembered having to wash in a tip-up bath in front of the fire. The more substantial cottages, those belonging to tradesmen and shopkeepers, might boast a copper for heating water, but most made do with a pan suspended over an open fire. Water came from wells, shared by all. The bucket and ropes were renewed every eight years or so, paid for by those who used them until parish councils took over the cost. Later they were replaced by street taps (Wool's remaining in use until the 1960s).

In his account of the annual migration from farm to farm for employment, Hardy described the furniture piled high on the waggon carrying a labourer's family to its new home. The dresser took pride of place, followed by barrels filled with crockery, a hive of bees, a cooking pot or crock packed with flower roots, while on top of the table and few wooden chairs 'a circular nest is made of the bed and bedding for the matron and children.' The mother held the clock, the eldest daughter was placed in charge of the mirror.

In 1874 a labourer's wages in the Marshwood Vale were 8 shillings a week, to which were added a free cottage, some cider, grist corn, a potato patch and coal and faggots. By the start of the First World War labour shortages had pushed up wages to about 12 shillings, leaving a few pence spare. To help spread the cost many families subscribed to Coal and Clothing Clubs.

As more food was imported, the diet improved. Bread and potatoes remained the staples, as well as small amounts of butter, cheese, bacon and tea. By 1900 the shelves of the village shop offered canned meat and sardines, as well as cocoa, margarine, treacle, syrup and jam. Mutton and beef allowed a break from the endless bacon or pieces of pork. A Board of Trade report of 1902 listed a Dorset labourer's weekly diet:

Breakfast – bread, butter, cheese, cold bacon, tea (Sundays, fried bacon).
Dinner – boiled bacon, potatoes and other vegetables (Sundays, mutton or beef, with pudding); or salt pork, vegetables, dumplings (Sundays, a little fresh meat or pork).
Tea – bread, butter or jam, cheese, tea (Sundays, cake).
Supper – very rarely any, or if any, vegetables and salt pork.

Most shopping took place in the village, but market days in the towns meant a regular weekly outing, usually in a carrier's cart. Goods were cheaper, the choice was greater. And in winter newly acquired street lamps in the larger villages welcomed those returning home with their shopping. The lamps ran on paraffin oil and were lit at

RODDEN ROW
ABBOTSBURY.

night, for which the lamplighter was paid £4 a year. Many villages started music groups or horticultural societies, and once recreation grounds were established football was played. Initially it was a novelty. Bere Regis Football Club, known as 'The Arabs', played its frst match in 1887, causing 'much amusement among the spectators, many of whom had never seen the game before.'

From 1900 onwards many parishes grouped together to form District Nursing Associations, employing a fully certified midwife, for which the villagers subscribed a shilling a year and an additional five shillings for attending a birth. For other cases labourers were charged 2d, tradespeople 4d, farmers 6d, whilst those 'on the parish' and in receipt of poor law relief were treated free. Herbs were widely used, especially in pregnancy. Remedies and cure-alls varied from village to village. In the Gussages, for example, goose grease was spread on brown paper and placed inside a vest for those with a weak chest.

Frederick Swaffield came to Stoke Abbott when he was seven in 1895, and many years later wrote an account of life there in the years before the First World War. It may

ABBOTSBURY. Looking east along Rodden Row from the junction with Market Street in about 1900. The building on the right was one of two tea rooms in the village, probably that of Mrs Susan Gee, 'baker, tea, coffee and refreshment rooms; refreshments at moderate charges. Today it is a private house, with its modern successor, Abbotsbury Tea Rooms, almost directly opposite.

be an old man's memories, only the good times recalled, but it has the ring of truth.

'There used to be a great number of men and boys employed on the farms. I have seen as many as forty or fifty turn out from the two pubs on a Saturday night from Laverstock, Brimley, Stoke Knapp and Bucks Head like a great family and discuss the week's work. They used to take such interest in their work, blacksmiths, carpenters, carters, shepherds, cowmen, hurdlemen, flaxdressers, rabbit-catchers, farmers and all. Since I have grown up and look back on the old days, village life seemed full of beauty: people were poor, but everybody seemed happy and everyone at work.'

The Lodge, Alderholt.

ALDERHOLT. Children gathered in Sandleheath Lane outside the entrance to Alderholt Park. The mid-19th century East Lodge was built at the same time as the house it served. When this photograph was taken Alderholt Park was lived in by George Churchill, a member of a wealthy Dorchester family, who remained its owner until after the First World War. The house was eventually separated from its 2,000 farming estate following a sale in 1986. The lodge remains, but not the freshly-painted railings or pond. The Park is on the border of three counties, allowing George Churchill to claim that he had flushed a duck in Dorset, shot it in Hampshire, and picked it up in Wiltshire.

ASHMORE. The village policeman stands in the bottom of an empty Ashmore pond in September 1911. The pond is at at least 300 hundred years old and is 16 feet deep at its deepest point. It rarely dries out, though only fed by rain, but the summer of 1911 – the so-called 'Halcyon Summer' – was one of the driest and warmest on record. There was hardly any rain from May onwards, and the drought finally broke on September 12th, shortly after this photograph was taken. The villagers traditionally hold a feast when the pond dries. Cakes are baked and eaten in the bed of the pond. In the old days local farmers used to haul out the cartloads of mud that gathered on the bottom for manuring their land.

ASHMORE POND. EMPTY. SEP. 1911. TYLER PHOTO.

Above: ASHMORE. Alfred and Annie Hiscock standing outside their cottage at Well Bottom, near the old track known as Gravely Lane. Altogether, there were nine cottages at Well Bottom, all built by squatters, whose right to occupy their sites was initially established by completing the chimney stack in a 24 hour period. Most have been demolished, including – alas – Alfred and Annie's modest brick and thatch cottage and one bought by the parish as the poorhouse. Alfred died in 1906 aged 78, and Annie, whose father was a shepherd from Tollard Royal, followed him aged 85 nine years later.

Below: BAGBER. The birthplace of the Dorset dialect poet William Barnes (1801-1886) was a hamlet of cob and thatch cottages with a few newer brick houses when this photograph was taken towards the end of the century. Despite the enclosure of Bagber Common in the 1830s, with the loss of the commoners' rights, it was still occupied by farm workers, dairymen and graziers. This view looks west along the A357. The two cottages on the left were built in 1872 near the junction with the lane to Bagber Common, but only the further one still stands, with a date and the initials of its owner picked out in bricks on the gable end.

Above: BLOXWORTH. In 1895, when this photograph of the hamlet of Newport was taken, the entire village and surrounding 3,000 acres were owned by the Pickard-Cambridge family, as they had been since 1751. Most villagers were either employed by the estate, or by its three tenant farmers. The population was about 270, of whom about 30 were children, but despite its size the village supported a blacksmith, grocer and draper, post office and school. Here the photographer has his back to the entrance gates to Bloxworth House. The cottage on the left, known as 'Ma Swyer's' survives, but both the tile-roofed forge and estate laundry opposite have been demolished. The cottages beyond were pulled down in the 1960s and rebuilt, but set further back from the lane. The cottage on the right burnt down.

Below: BOVINGTON. The High Street in about 1910. In 1896 the War Department purchased of 100 acres of heath for £4,300 from the Frampton family of Moreton for use as a 'Rifle Range or for any other Military Use or purpose'. The land was poor, but the Spicer family had a small dairy and eked out a precarious living. Not suprisingly, it was they who first profited from the arrival of 1,000 soldiers in June 1900, opening 'Bovington Drug Stores' in a hastily thrown up tin building. Initially, accommodation was in a tented camp, but so many battalions made use of the ranges that the tents were gradually replaced by huts.

"THE DOCTOR'S VISIT"   Copyright.

BULBARROW. What is surely one of the most remarkable of all Dorset postcards. Doctor Fielding and Nurse Marlowe attending a gypsy birth in April 1906, one of the 17 children born to Lavinia and Arthur Hughes, a 'rat-and-varmint destroyer'.

Thanks to their work in collecting traditional travellers' songs by the celebrated folk singers Ewan MacColl and Peggy Seeger (*Travellers' Songs from England and Scotland*, 1977) more than usual is known about the Hughes family, who were part of an extended Romany community that travelled widely throughout Dorset and settled on Canford Heath prior to it being built on – and still flourish today.

Another child, Caroline, born in a horse-drawn caravan in Bere Regis in 1900, became a well-known singer, as was her mother. 'My mother sang all the time. When she were making clothes-pegs or making we children's bloomers, shifts and petticoats. We be all around the fire singing these old songs,

and I been with my mother listening, listening, and I made her sing them over and over until I learned the lot.'

Caroline, like all the daughters, went hawking with her mother from the age of ten. 'Where are you going to find a good mother when she's gone? One who's worked, slaved hard, runned and raced for you, been through bitter frost and snow, finding snitches of wood, buckets of water, through all the ups and downs.' Caroline never learnt to read, and went on to have eight children and 35 grandchildren herself.

The National Archives hold recordings of her singing, though a double CD of her songs, issued by the Living Tradition, *Sheep-Crook and Black Dog*, is no longer available. As Queen Caroline Hughes she died in 1971 and was given a traditional gypsy funeral, in which her 'caravan and all her possessions were burnt in the presence of her tribe.'

I long to know what persuaded the photographer to go all the way to Bulbarrow in order to take this photograph.

BRADFORD PEVERELL. Church Cottages in Muckleford Lane in about 1890, when estate servants were often lodged in them. Harold Gill, who was born in the village and now lives in what was the old shop, spent much of his childhood in the nearest of the cottages, all three of which were bought by his father for a princely £25 in the early 1950s. Built of flint, rubble and chalk bound together with cob, they were eventually condemned and demolished, and much of the site is now occupied by various garages.

BURTON BRADSTOCK. A van from Bridport Model Laundry making its rounds on Barr Lane in the early 1920s. The two villas on the clifftop, Alpha and Beta, were built between 1885 and 1890 as summer residences for the Pitt-Rivers family, who owned much of the village until 1958 (when the right hand one sold for £3,800). One is now the Seaside Boarding House, the other the home of the musician Billy Bragg and his wife. Commercial steam laundries and improvements in transport removed a traditional source of extra income for women in many Dorset villages. In 1881 Burton Bradstock had five laundresses, by 1927 there were none.

BURTON BRADSTOCK. Southover – known as the Street of Mariners – with the whitewashed Dove Inn on the left. Although the Dove closed in 2000 and has been converted into two dwellings, little else has changed, and all but the cottage on the left still remain thatched. Six others were destroyed by fire on a September evening in 1898. One victim was a Mrs Hussey, who had just said her prayers and was heading for bed when her thatch caught alight. The cottages in the photograph were only saved by the quick-thinking village policeman, P.C. Hansford, who organised a human chain of buckets of water. Two months later the schooner *Flirt* was wrecked on the cliffs at the end of the lane. A local fisherman saved one man, but the rest all drowned, and the bodies were laid out in the 'mortuary' shed opposite the inn. The *Flirt*'s hatch was washed ashore, and made into a table for the Dove.

Below: CATTISTOCK. Duck Street in 1880. The village was virtually self-sufficient, supporting four grocers, two blacksmiths, two tailors, three boot and shoe makers, and a butcher – as well as millers, carpenters and wheelwrights. Evidence of the complete rebuilding of the church tower in 1875 can be seen in the fresh Ham and Portland stonework. It cost £3,000 and was the gift of the rector, H. Keith Barnes. After the Second World War it was rebuilt again, having been destroyed by fire in 1940. Note the gas lamps. Just visible on the left is the school (closed 1980) with its bell tower. This same view now includes the Tudor-style Savill Hall, a memorial to Frank Savill of Chantmarle Manor who died of his wounds in 1916 and is buried in the churchyard.

Above: CERNE ABBAS. Acreman Street in 1892, now the main Dorchester/Sherborne road, showing a long demolished row of cob and thatch cottages. The entire street was widened and realigned in 1960 to keep traffic away from the centre of the village, but it was once the poorest part. Cerne's decline from town to village began with the loss of its fairs and silk mills, partly a knock-on response to being overlooked by the railway network. Yet worse times lay ahead. By 1923 the population had fallen to 511 (from a high of 1343 in 1851). Roofs had fallen in, walls had collapsed, cottages and workshops had disappeared, grass grew in the streets, 'pigs lived on the ground floors of the houses in Abbey Street, the then vicar's wife, singing ribaldry, drove a herd of white goats up the street, as her husband conducted his service in the church.'

Below: CERNE ABBAS. Cerne Union Workhouse opened on the edge of the village in 1837 to house and provide employment for 'able-bodied paupers'. The initial 109 inmates ranged from 'bedridden folk on blankets' to 'young women with their illegitimate babies' – as well as the 'simple-minded, the homeless and workless' – all of them drawn from the surrounding 20 parishes. The origins of England's workhouses stem from a report of 1834 in which Boards of Guardians were elected to take over the administration of poor relief, with neighbouring parishes being grouped together into a 'Union'. They remained controversial until their closure (Cerne Union closed in 1940 and has since been converted into flats) and the shame and fear attached to being sent to the workhouse blighted many lives.

CHEDINGTON. The village cricket club in 1907. The most remarkable thing about this photograph is that Chedington could even field a team. It is one of Dorset's smallest villages, and 1891 had a total population of 112, of whom a quarter were children. It is possible that the team was the private creation of the then owner of Chedington Court, Sir Henry Peto, the son of a Victorian railway magnate, who bought the estate in 1893. Cricket was popular throughout the county, with the formation of village teams once land was found for a pitch. A typical example is Bere Regis, founded in 1904 and captained by the vicar, with a pavilion being built a few years later. By 1909 its club members sported green and white caps and matching ties, and a flag was flown when a match was in progress.

CHICKERELL. West Street from North Square, with the blacksmith's forge on the right. The house beyond it still stands and is largely unchanged, but a modern house occupies the site of the forge. The population in 1891 was 818 (in 2011 it was 5,515). The heart of the village lies well inland, but it extends south down to the Fleet and Chesil Beach, so that seasonal mackerel fishing was an important source of income, as was brickmaking.

CORFE CASTLE. West Street and the Castle, 1890. Until the 18th century this was the principal thoroughfare, and was once lined with workshops where stone from Purbeck's quarries was worked and then taken to Ower Quay on Poole Harbour to be shipped. By the date of this photograph East Street was the main road through the village and West Street had become a down-at-heel backwater ending at Corfe Common.

DEWLISH. A view of the village from the lane to Milborne St Andrew. In the centre, on Middle Street, is Parsonage Farm with its ancillary barn and farm buildings. Prominent on the bend is the Wesleyan Chapel, rebuilt in 1859 following the disastrous fire of the previous year which began in Dewlish Brewery, destroyed 23 cottages and cost the life of a four-year-old boy. Such was the local opposition to NonConformity when the chapel was built the original entrance was hidden to one side, where the boot scraper can still be seen. This photograph must have been taken after 1905. By then the congregation had won round its detractors and was sufficiently confident to rebuild the front with a door facing the road. Like the thatched barns in the background, the two lines of elms on the right are no longer standing.

EAST KNIGHTON. This is as bleak an image of rural life in late 19th century Dorset as any in the book. 'What is to become of the poor Dorset labourers?' asked an M.P. in 1899, and the impact of the agricultural depression and the depopulation that followed is all to clear in these cottages. Those on the left still stand, those on the right have been demolished. The building in the background was the forge, whose site on the busy A352 is now occupied by Rainbow Garage.

The Village, E. Knighton.

GIPSY'S CAMP, EYPE DOWN, BRIDPORT.

EYPE. Gypsies camped on Eype Down. Dorset had a large gypsy and Romany community, of whom the most noted families were Hughes (see page 41), Benhams, Coopers, and Whites. Some were travelling hawkers whose horse-drawn caravans followed a seasonal route round the county, selling everything from ribbons and bales of cloth to pots and pans. The women often cut clothes pegs or wove baskets. The men sharpened tools, or took casual jobs helping bring in the harvest or as charcoal burners. Few stayed in one place for long. A residential gypsy school opened by a well-meaning local rector in Farnham in 1847 lasted a mere eight years, later becoming the Pitt-Rivers Museum and now converted into housing.

FARNHAM. The village well was housed in this sturdy late Victorian building at the expense of General Augustus Pitt Rivers, whose Rushmore Estate included Farnham. It still stands, largely unaltered, at the entrance to the churchyard.

FIFEHEAD NEVILLE. A lad leading a water cart and various other villagers pose for the photographer at the little 6 ft wide packhorse bridge that crosses the River Divelish. The bridge's date is uncertain, but it possibly dates back to medieval times.

old Bridge Fifehead Neville.

Above: FONTMELL MAGNA. The elm in the foreground was known as the Cross Tree or Gossip Tree and had been planted on the site of a market cross in the 18th century. Sadly, it fell victim to Dutch Elm Disease and was replaced by a lime in 1977, the year of Queen Elizabeth II's Jubilee. The line of cottages in the background is now a single house.

Below: FRAMPTON. Villagers gathered outside their cottages opposite the lane leading to Southover. Kelly's *Directory* describes it as 'formerly a market town', but by the date of this photograph in 1880 it had become an estate village owned in its entirety by Richard and Marcia Sheridan, who lived at Frampton Court. They were popular landlords, paying for a reading room, a home for the homeless, and funding the village school. Richard Sheridan's death in 1888 marked the high point in the family's fortunes. Extravagance, the death of an heir in the First World War, and the belief of the last of the family, Clare, in an ancient curse that no first-born son would ever inherit the estate, led to its entire 7,000 acres being put up for auction in 1931, after which Frampton Court was demolished, leaving only the servants' wing.

FROME ST QUINTIN.

GLANVILLES WOOTTON APRIL 14TH 1907

TREE STRUCK BY LIGHTNING.

Above: FROME ST QUINTIN. Although squeezed between the A37 and the main Weymouth/Bristol line, the gentle unhurried character of this late 19th century photograph of the south end of the village still remains true today. What is now Manor Farm is on the right, whilst Frome House lies behind the wall on the left. The coachman patiently waits for the two women and the photographer to tire of their afternoon in the countryside.

Left: GLANVILLES WOOTTON. Posed for the photographer amidst the remnants of a tree struck by lightning on April 14 1907.

Left: HINTON ST MARY. Looking south towards the centre of the village from the road to Marnhull in November 1909.

Ibberton.

Elsworth, Ibberton.

Above: IBBERTON. Looking north up the lane to the church in about 1910. Solomon Elsworth was the village carrier, and the photograph was probably taken to publicise his services at a time when the motorcar was just beginning to threaten his trade. Like most Blackmore Vale villages, Ibberton was staunchly NonConformist. At the date of this photograph the parish church was roofless and disused. Although there was a small corrugated-iron Anglican church, religious life centred on the chapels of the Primitive Methodists and Wesleyans. Here, the surviving Wesleyan Chapel of 1884 is visible at the top end of the lane, but much else has changed. The neatly thatched village shop and post office on the left has been demolished, as has half the cottage on the right. The half that remains is now a pub, aptly named The Ibberton.

Below: LANGTON HERRING. Looking north along Shop Lane in about 1910. The village is the only 'Thankful Village' in Dorset, and one of only 52 in Great Britain to have suffered no fatalities amongst those who served in the First World War. Even more remarkably, it is one of only 13 'Doubly Thankful' villages, losing no one in the Second World either. The gate on the right led to the bakery, whilst the post office was run by the carrier, Thomas Whittle. The population was under 300, the men earning a living by fishing or working on its two farms.

LYDLINCH COMMON. Croft House is on the left, Blackmore Farm on the right. Just visible behind protective railings on the grass is the oak tree planted in September 1902 by Lady Barbara Yeatman-Biggs to mark the Coronation of Edward VII. Lady Barbara was the wife of Huyshe Yeatman-Biggs, owner of Stock Gaylard and its celebrated deer park. Although then Bishop of Southwark (and later Bishop of Worcester), Huyshe had been forced to rescue the estate from its creditors by buying it from his widowed sister-in-law. Well over a century later the railings have gone, but the oak stands, now fully grown and majestic. The school log book recorded its planting, first noting 'Reggie Lane away with measles': following an address by the Bishop 'the children marched to the Common where the ceremony took place. They then sang "Three Cheers for the Red, White and Blue", "God Save the King", "Here's a Health unto his Majesty".

LYTCHETT MATRAVERS. David McDonald and Violet Marsh drawing water from the well in 1913 at what is now known as Parish Well Corner, the junction of Eldons Drove and Middle Road, with South House and its stable on the right. In 1958 the well was replaced by a hand pump on the roadside. The pump ended up at Spy Farm, and in 1981 after being given to the parish it was put back on the Corner by funds provided by the Womens Institute. Despite its proximity to Poole, early 20th century Lytchett consisted of about 40 smallholdings and farms, few much more than 50 acres. The population was 700: in 2011 it was 3,500.

Above: MAIDEN NEWTON. The Irish-born Sergeant of Police, John Simpson, with his wife Alice and some of his four children outside the police station on the Dorchester road: it later moved, finally closing in the 1980s. Under the terms of an act of 1856 all counties throughout the British Isles were required to establish a County Constabulary under a Chief Constable for the rural areas. By the end of the century all the larger villages had their own police station, with drunkenness and poaching the most common offences. One of the glories of the Dorset force is the 'Black Book' issued to all new constables, of which these are two samples:

  Q: If you saw a person about to commit a serious crime, what should you do?
  A: Prevent, if possible, and apprehend him.
  Q: How should you walk when in charge of a prisoner?
  A: On one side, about half a pace to the rear, so as to prevent him tripping me up.

Remarkably, the book remained in use until the 1930s

Opposite page top: MELBURY OSMOND. Looking up The Street from the Watersplash and Packhorse Bridge. The semi-detached cottage on the left was built in 1794, and although unnamed was known as the 'House of Steps' (it remains largely unchanged and is now Riverside Cottages). The woman in the doorway is probably Fanny Pitcher, whose husband Frank was from a large well-known Melbury family. All the surrounding land and just under half the houses in the village are owned by the Ilchester Estate. Thomas Hardy's mother was born in the village, and married in its church.

Opposite page bottom: MILBORNE ST ANDREW. Dorchester Hill, with the Royal Oak Inn just visible on the right. B. Baker was the village grocer. The white stag outside Stag House on the left was a gift to a Mr Cole by John Sawbridge Erle-Drax, MP for Wareham until 1880, for his support in an election campaign. Erle-Drax, who lived at Charborough Park, was known as the 'Silent MP'. His only statement in the House was a request that a window be opened. Following his death he was buried in the Byzantine mausoleum he designed for himself at Holnest. It included a letter box in which *The Times* was delivered daily. Sadly, the mausoleum was demolished in 1935.

MELBURY OSMOND. 6.

B.BAKER
PROVISION
MERCHANT

Above: MORECOMBELAKE. 'The Sports'.

Below: PIDDLEHINTON. Children gathered on the bridge in about 1900. Much of the village was owned by Eton College, who had been given it by Henry VI in 1440 (they sold both land and cottages in 1966). The children will have gone to the village school, which opened in 1862 and closed in 1981. Today, they go to the modern Piddle Valley Church of England First School in Piddletrenthide. A century earlier, in 1881, overcrowding led the rector asking for government funding for a second classroom on the grounds that: 'the interest in education is so slack in our little country village.'

PIDDLETRENTHIDE. The High Street in about 1912, with the post office and village shop on the left. The building opposite was a seed merchants, whose owner Charles Groves is standing in its entrance. The Groves family went on to combine selling seeds with a successful nursery and market garden on the steep ground behind the house. The man in the lane on the right was a local tramp known as 'Budgen', whilst further back on the right Charles Hunt stands outside the forge.

PIDDLETRENTHIDE. This area, known as Egypt, marked the original route between Dorchester and the villages strung along the Piddle Valley, with another lane heading east towards the church. No one knows the origins of the name, though it has been suggested that it is because gypsies once camped in the area. The cottages on the left no longer stand.

PIDDLETRENTHIDE. Describing the house on the left many years later, the writer and broadcaster Ralph Wightman wrote, 'I was born on the 26th July 1901, in a house called "Riverside" with a butcher's shop on one end. The front door of the house opened directly on the village street, which was the main road, and the back wall rose directly from the stream, which in flood time flowed through the back door and out the front. Drinking water had to be fetched in a bucket from the village pump about forty yards away. My parents were a bit fussy about this drinking water, but I remember a leathery and healthy old lady just below us who was to content to fill her kettle from the river. But I also remember our butcher's shop and slaughterhouse!'

The shop and houses were later demolished for road widening, as were the thatched cottages opposite. Mains water finally replaced the pump in about 1938.

PIMPERNE.

New Street, Piddletown.

Opposite page top: PIMPERNE. Looking east along Salisbury Road in about 1910, with the old forge set back on the left. Note the line of elms. Until it was auctioned in 1924 the entire village was owned by the Portman Estate. The card was written from Blandford Camp in 1915, whose wooden huts were hastily thrown up during the first winter of the war to house the Royal Naval Division.

Opposite page bottom: PORTESHAM. Back Street in about 1890. Most men in the village worked on one of the two principal farms, whilst their wives stayed at home braiding nets – helped after school and in the evenings by their daughters. James Jolliffe, a carrier and shopkeeper, acted as agent for one of the Bridport netmaking companies, collecting various thicknesses of twine once a week for distribution to the villagers. As well as seine-nets, they made black-tarred brussel sprout nets, for which they earned 3 shillings a hundred, partly paid in groceries from Jolliffe's shop. The tin bath would have been used for the weekly bath in front of the fire.

Above: PUDDLETOWN (Note the old un-tidied up spelling on the card). New Street. In the introduction to the 1895 edition of *Far from the Madding Crowd*, much of which is set in a thinly disguised Puddletown, Hardy regretted the pulling down of most of its cob and thatch cottages, with their brick floors and small windows. Thirty years earlier Ilsington House and virtually the whole of Puddletown was bought by John Brymer, originally a hatter, who rose to become High Sheriff of Dorset. Brymer systematically demolished the cottages in the centre of the village as their leases fell in and replaced them with three terraces in the then fashionable Gothic style.

Below: SANDFORD ORCAS. Lower Sandford in 1905, with the schoolhouse at the end of the street. The man in the centre was George Brine, the village blacksmith and carrier, who took over from his father, also George. The pony and trap belonged to the younger George, which he used for taking people to Sherborne and back, charging 2s 6d for the journey inclusive of waiting for an hour whilst they did their shopping. Dairy Cottage on the left was demolished in about 1950.

RAMPISHAM. Looking towards the centre of the village with Beers Cottage on the left. All the buildings on the right were demolished after the Second World War. They had been built on a spring line, and fell victim to rising damp. The message on the back of the card takes a more optimistic view of Rampisham's prospects: 'Thought you might like this to add to your collection. What do you think of it? Don't you think Rampisham is looking up.'

SHROTON. Villagers gathered outside Ivy Porch Cottages in about 1890, with the village school and post office in the background. Writing ten years earlier about the village's ownership by 'an active and prominent member of the House of Commons', a visitor observed that 'building operations on an extensive scale were proceeding, the evident intention being to provide the maximum of good cottage accommodation for the peasantry of the district.'

Above: SIXPENNY HANDLEY. The High Street in the early 1900s, after it had been rebuilt following the fire of May 1892. On the right is a rare and happily still flourishing country butcher, W.S. Clarke & Sons. Frederick Treves 1906 description of the village as the 'ugliest' in Dorset is unfair, for he was writing when much of it was being rebuilt in red brick following the fire, which began in the blacksmith's forge and left the heart of the village in ruins. The Methodist chapel and 46 cottages were destroyed, leaving 186 people homeless, 'the greater portion losing everything even down to their clothing.'

Below: SIXPENNY HANDLEY. The Common Pond in about 1890, with the parish church in the background. The Common lay north of the village, over which local smallholders had the right to graze livestock and gather furze and kindling. The Pond was once much larger than in the photograph, providing water for stock, punting in summer and ice skating in winter for the village children. It was initially filled in when mains water arrived, then dug out by the Scouts and lined with plastic. Today it is a small dishevelled wildlife haven, rich in flag irises and frogs.

Above: SOUTH PERROTT. Looking east down the Main Street, with the first post office in one of the cottages on the right. In 1891 the population was 250, of whom 122 were born in the village – a statistic unimaginable today. The men were mostly farm workers, supported by two innkeepers, a grocer, baker, wheelwright, road mender, carpenter, shoemaker, two blacksmith, and stone mason. For women the choices were between dressmaking, laundry work, or domestic service. Although the line of cottages survive, many have been demolished for road-widening schemes – despite which the road through the village remains narrow and the traffic on the A356 is still a hazard.

Below: SPETISBURY. Looking down on the village from near the railway line. The fine entrance pillars with a gas lamp over them led to the Congregational Chapel. The card was posted in 1904 to a Miss Hooper in Wallis Down (then two words) and on the back is written: 'Dear S. Mr Hunt committed suicide this morning (Thursday) by drowning himself. Awful isn't it? Hope you are alright. Saw Mrs H this morning. With love Amy.' Robert Hunt was the well-known village shopkeeper, as well as Overseer of the Poor and involved in the Temperance Movement. As he became older, he grew mentally unstable. Reporting his death, the *East Dorset Herald* noted that he had been 'despondent for some months'. (see page 91).

SPETISBURY. Sloper's Mead, the centre of the village, before and after the fire of May 18th 1905. Despite the absence of a sign or any advertisements, the thatched house with the drawn shutters on the right was a shop (it survived the fire). The fire began in a bakery in the morning and soon spread across the road, destroying the blacksmith's house and several cottages. 'The heat was so great that for a time one side of the village was cut off from the other, but everyone who could helped with a will to rescue as much of the furniture as was possible before the roofs fell in.' None of those made homeless were insured, and one family was left with only the clothes they stood up in. There was a certain amount of recrimination afterwards. Blandford fire engine's pump didn't work properly, whilst Wimborne's two horses were insufficient to pull the two-ton engine, thus taking an hour to arrive. The Drax Estate built the baker Bertram Andrews a new bakery, which continued under different owners until the 1980s.

Above: STOBOROUGH. Boys playing marbles in the lane in about 1880, looking north towards Wareham. Thanks to the opening of the Wareham bypass a century later Stoborough's traffic is much reduced, and if nimble enough a game of marbles might again be possible. The cottages on the right still stand, though with dormer windows and tiled roofs replacing the thatch.

Below: STOUR PROVOST. High Street, 1909. Apart from the loss of thatch for all but the cottage in the background this view has changed little, partly because the village remains compact and quiet on what is essentially a no-through road. Notice the string tied round the trousers of the man on the left, and the birdcage over the door of what is now called Provost House. Keeping a canary was common at the time; even Fancy Day in *Under the Greenwood Tree* had one. The bay window of the shop (see also page 93) is just visible behind the man by the milk churn. The house with the railings in front, No 5, had various incarnations as an inn, forge and police station. The village owes its name to the Provost and Fellows of King's College, Cambridge, who were given it by Edward IV in the late 15th century (sold 1925). The card was written in the morning, posted in Putney and delivered to an address in Mortlake in the afternoon.

Above: SYDLING ST NICHOLAS. Cottages on Back Street in about 1890. Until the 1950s virtually the entire village and over 4,000 acres of land belonged to Winchester College, whose bursar came twice a year to collect the rent (farmhouses 2/6d a week, cottages 1/-). In return the College provided free thatch and laid on an annual tenants lunch at the Greyhound Inn. The sad state of the cottages in the photograph reflects the falling population, which went from 563 to 414 in the ten years before 1901. This view has changed considerably, and there are now gaps where many of the cottages once stood, including all those immediately to the right of the bridge.

Below: SYDLING ST NICHOLAS. Sarah Newberry collecting water outside Ham Farm in about 1900. Sarah and her husband Charles tenanted Ham Farm in 1889, and the Newberry family remained in the village until the 1950s. The water-powered Upper Mill (demolished 1950), stood opposite, its flow regulated by hatches. All water in the village came from wells or the Sydling Brook until a street-piped supply was installed in 1932, but another 20 years went by before it was piped directly into the cottages and houses. The weir and its pool no longer survive, supposedly because the noise kept people awake.

Above: THORNCOMBE. Looking up Fore Street outside the bakery in about 1905. The woman wearing an apron beneath the window was Elizabeth Bailey, whose family owned the bakery until 1930. Like Trent (once in Somerset), Thorncombe was an isolated enclave of another county. Various electoral and ecclesiastical changes in the 1830s transferred the Devon parish to a Dorset parliamentary district and from the Diocese of Exeter to that of Salisbury, culminating in an Act of 1844 which placed detached bits of counties to the 'Counties in which they are situate.'

Below: THORNCOMBE. Children gathered in Fore Street in 1890, with Chard Road off to the right leading to where the village shop is now. Just visible on the left is the Gospel Hall of 1881, which still flourishes today. At the top of the street is one of the village's three pubs, the Golden Lion. Alfred Cox was its landlord when in May 1882, eight years earlier, much of the village was destroyed by fire. 'Houses were burning in all directions and the villagers were in the wildest confusion and consternation,' wrote one witness to the blaze. The thatched Golden Lion was only saved by a human chain throwing buckets of water over the roof each time it caught fire. The pub closed in 1970 and today is a private house, Golden House.

Above: THROOP. A view of the hamlet on the lane leading downhill from Throop Clump in about 1900, with Well Cottage on the left. Throop is east of Briantspuddle on the River Piddle and remains largely unchanged. The forge was in the cottage on the right, with Throop Manor House and its chimneys opposite. Much of the hamlet had belonged to the Framptons of Moreton from the late 17th century until 1914, when it was bought by Ernest Debenham and added to the Bladen Estate.

Below: WINTERBORNE HOUGHTON. The horse-drawn van belonged to William Dicker from Winterborne Whitechurch. He was renowned for his sausages, which he delivered to the surrounding villages and came from the pigs on his smallholding. The photograph dates to about 1906, and the far row of thatched cottages no longer stands.

Top: WINTERBORNE KINGSTON. The Reading Room in 1905. It was paid for by John Mansel-Pleydell of Whatcombe, the local landowner, and the site is now occupied by the village hall and a bus stop. Mansel-Pleydell founded the Dorset Natural History & Archaeological Society, whose home is the Dorset County Museum. A number of Dorset villages had reading rooms, usually in places were the Liberal and Chapel movements were strong. Books and papers were provided. Soft drinks were available, helping encourage their use as a village meeting place at a time when excessive drinking in public houses was causing concern.

Centre: WINTERBOURNE STEEPLETON. The South Winterborne rises in springs just north of the village, and the cottages shown here in about 1890 have been rebuilt on slightly higher ground to avoid flooding. This postcard was hand-coloured, offering a carefully posed and idealized portrait of rural life.

Bottom: WINTERBORNE STICKLAND. A view of the allotments at the north end of the village in 1905. All have since been built on or returned to farmland, but the cottages are still standing. The provision of allotments was an important means of helping labourers put food on the table. In due course it became a political weapon, and the Liberals 'Three Acres and a Cow' slogan in the 1885 Election helped sweep them to power in all but one of Dorset's four constituencies. Legislation compelled trustees of charity lands to provide allotments, and local councils were given powers to compulsory purchase land for the purpose. By 1913 two-thirds of all villages had allotments, whose two most important crops were the potato and the pig. One Dorset landowner noted that 'the contented grunt of a fattening pig is pleasanter to the agricultural labourer's ear than the delicious notes of the sweetest nightingale.' In *Lark Rise to Candleford* Flora Thompson recalled that 'during its lifetime the pig was an important member of the family, and its health and condition were regularly reported in letters to children away from home.' The potatoes were traditionally planted on Good Friday.

WINTERBORNE ST MARTIN (Martinstown). The line of newly thatched cottages has since been demolished and is now a garden. On the left is the bridleway to Friar Waddon, with its cast iron sign of 1828 threatening 'transportation for life' if the bridge over the South Winterborne was damaged.

Right: WITCHAMPTON. The Victorian almshouses with their distinctive chimney stacks in about 1890. The six almshouses were for widows of workers on the 18,000 acre Crichel Estate, then owned by Humphrey Sturt, the 1st Lord Alington.

Below: WONSTON. This view of the small Blackmore Vale village near Hazelbury Bryan is remarkably unchanged. The photograph was taken by a member of the Mitchell family, possibly Joseph, who as well as being a plumber ran the village shop and post office seen here behind the bicycle on the left. In due course the post office moved, and the Mitchell family ran the shop as a general hardware and ironmongery, later opening a garage whose petrol pumps stood on the lane. The house burnt down in 1942, but was rebuilt and remains thatched to this day. Behind the wall on the right is Brewery Farm, beyond which lay a line of cottages, known as the Barracks, which have since been demolished.

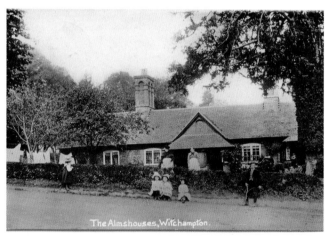

The Almshouses, Witchampton.

Wonstone, Hazelbury Bryan.

Mitchell
Hazelbury Bryan.

Above: WOOL. A view of the unusually wide High Street and road to West Lulworth in about 1900, with cows being brought in for milking. Charles Podger's bakery/grocery on the right later became the post office, which it still remains. The impact of the purchase of the surrounding heath by the War Department in 1896 has yet to be felt. The road through the village was surfaced with tarmac in 1921. Electricity followed four years later, but mains water only replaced the dozen or so taps placed around the village in 1877 nearly a century later, in the 1960s. The stream that once flowed down the street has since been filled in, whilst front gardens and a pavement have reduced the width of the street.

Below: WORTH MATRAVERS. The pond in about 1890, its bank eroded by the cattle from Worth Manor Farm pausing for a drink. Beyond it on the extreme left is the little village school, now closed. The village is one of only a handful where farming took second place to another source of employment. Most men worked in the quarries, either underground in the coastal quarries at Winspit and Seacombe, or in one of the scattered small-scale workings that dot the limestone plateau behind the village. The cottage beyond the pond was the home of James Lowe, a cobbler who made 'straights', boots that could be worn on either foot.

UPWEY. The members of the Rifle Club in 1907.

YETMINSTER. The small farms and cottages comprising Brister End lay slightly outside the centre of the village on the far side of the railway line. The railway's arrival in 1857 was followed by the opening of a milk factory, and the brick terrace of Victorian workers cottages on the right may well date to the same period. The cottages survive, but the two on the immediate right have been demolished, and the yard on the left adjoining the 17th century Sussex Farm House is now open ground.

CHURCH, CHAPEL &
THE TEMPERANCE MOVEMENT

STOUR ROW. The little Congregational Chapel on the lane to Todber is now the
Village Hall. NonConformity in the village dates back to 1838, when the
Rev T. Evans from Shaftesbury began holding services in what was then a butcher's
shop. The chapel opened five years later. Its pastor for 40 years was
William England Dennis, who died in 1895.

Perhaps the most visible rural legacy of Victorian Dorset are its NonConformist chapels. Usually of brick and slate, sturdily built yet modest, with no unnecessary architectural airs and graces – much like the men and women who once worshipped in them – they stand as testimony to widespread discontent with the established church during the latter half of the 19th century.

Macaulay's jibe that the Church of England was the 'Tory party at prayer' was self-evident in a county of large landowning estates, where traditional attitudes of paternalism and deference were taken for granted. Squire and parson shared similar social backgrounds. The squire often held the living, with the right to decide who occupied its rectory. Witchampton's rector for 67 years, the Rev Carr Glyn, was a younger son of the local landowner (he died aged 98, still in harness). Even the internal layout of most parish churches affirmed the gulf between the rulers and the ruled. Pews were usually rented, with the gentry occupying those at the front, the labourers and their families sitting on benches in the side aisles or back of the nave.

Thanks to the deep pockets of the new breed of Victorian landowners, whose wealth came from outside the county, many Dorset churches were either restored or completely rebuilt, alas often at the expense of their original character and fittings. The parson's influence extended from the pulpit into all corners of village life, from its school to the payment of tithes. They were magistrates, controlled charities, administered the hated Poor Law, taught Sunday School. The autocratic rector of Trent, Rev W. H. Turner, insisted that his parishioners bowed or curtsied to his carriage, even when empty.

Of course there were many exceptions. The best Victorian churches are the equal of any: Kingston and Cattistock are examples. The same is true of their incumbents. The Rev Octavius Pickard of Bloxworth deliberately had the box pews removed to stress the equality of all in the sight of god. The much-loved rector of Winterborne Came, the Dorset dialect poet William Barnes, walked up to fifteen miles a day to visit his parishioners until well into his late seventies, as did Henry Carver at Melbury Abbas, though not on foot but in a pony and trap. The Rev Sydney Godolphin Osborne of Durweston harangued *The Times* in innumerable letters to draw attention to the appalling living conditions of Dorset rural labourers.

Osborne's Christian Socialism was a first cousin to NonConformity, 'to preach the truth boldly'. Dissenting worship was usually inspired by one individual, a local preacher with the talent to attract followers from amongst his neighbours – usually craftsmen, tradesmen and small farmers. Thomas Gabe was Thornford's blacksmith, who once 'done with drinking and swearing' became a leading Methodist on the north Dorset circuit. Meetings were initially held in private houses until there were sufficient followers and funds to build a chapel. Land was often given, usually on the edge of a village. The materials for the Methodist chapel at Gussage All Saints were transported to the site on farm waggons by the various families involved.

There were fêtes, tea meetings and annual outings, providing a sense of fellowship and community, specially amongst families moving from parish to parish in search of employment. Women played a central role in chapel life, as at Bere Regis where it owed much to the 'godly life and devout services of faithful women'. Importance was placed on self-improvement and self-help. 'They were good, honest, hard-working people, very poor, devout in worship, rich in the simple things of life and in nature,' wrote Bernard Marsh, recalling his Methodist childhood in Dewlish. A flourishing chapel and resounding hymn singing was proof that a rich social and spiritual life could be gained independently of the parish church and its hierarchy.

NonConformists were by conviction more political than their Anglican brethren, allying themselves to such causes as the agricultural labourers trades union movement of the 1870s, the extension of the franchise, and the suffrage and Temperance Movements. The refusal of the Church of England to relinquish its hold over elementary education or allow NonConformist ministers to conduct a funeral service in a churchyard were other battles it ultimately won.

Yet whether Catholic, Wesleyan or Anglican, the agricultural depression of the *Lost Dorset* years left its mark on both church and chapel. Many were too big and badly maintained. As populations fell, so too did the influence of the Church of England on rural life. From 1869 the rector of Gussage St Michael was the Rev Joseph Ward. Together with his wife, and on an annual stipend of £200, he brought up four children, employed four maids, a gardener, and a governess for his daughters. But Ward was almost the last of a breed and the gentleman parson with private means soon gave way to a salaried clergyman unable to keep the roof on his once elegant Georgian rectory. The world in which Thomas Hardy's grandfather played the cello in Stinsford church band was replaced by the solemn tones of the organ. The church was still the place for baptisms, weddings and funerals, but the pews were beginning to empty – rarely to be full again.

ALDERHOLT. The Ebenezer Congregational Chapel at Cripplestyle stood down a dead-end track that opened out onto the heath and rough grazing. It stood alone, far from the village, as did most early NonConformist chapels. It opened in 1807, and 'the work was done chiefly by the people themselves. After the day's ordinary toil was over, they set to, the men digging and working the clay, and the women gathering heather from the common to bind it together.' As the congregation grew, sometimes reaching 200, the chapel was twice extended. Despite efforts to save the building, it finally collapsed in 1976 and the site is now marked by a stone memorial. By the date of this photograph its days as a place of worship were drawing to a close. In 1888 a replacement chapel was built on a new site facing Daggons Road, and that too has now closed. This is one of the earliest postcards in the book, and may date to the 1860s. The man on the right could be Samuel Williams, the minister for 40 years until his death in 1882, possibly with his wife and some of his five children.

ASHMORE. The Mission Hall in Green Lane, shortly after it opened in 1904. There was also a Methodist Chapel in the village. One preacher lived further down Green Lane at Well Bottom, whilst another walked over from Tollard Royal. Both buildings have been converted into dwellings.

BROADMAYNE. The annual meeting of Broadmayne Temperance Society outside Fryer Mayne Manor in about 1900. The Temperance Movement flourished in Victorian Britain. In 1900 there were 100,000 pubs (in 2017 there were 52,000). Beer was cheap and free of tax, drunkenness widespread. Initially, the founders of the movement saw the campaign against alchohol as a way of proving that working-class people were responsible enough to be given the vote. Later it came to be associated with NonConformity and progressive politics, particularly female suffrage. Many in the photograph are wearing the white ribbon, the symbol of the women's temperance movement. The band was the Broadmayne Salvation Army Band, whose Citadel was at the Dorchester end of the village.

CORFE MULLEN. The original village lay round round the medieval parish church of St Hubert, though the only significant buildings to have survived are the church, mill, Coventry Arms and Court House. The cob and thatch cottage in the photograph, with its brick extension, stood alongside the Higher Blandford Road, originally a late 18th century turnpike between Poole and Blandford, and now the road leading to the modern village. The cottage has gone, possibly demolished following the opening of the Broadstone single track railway cut off in 1886, which passed within a few yards. Its site remains undeveloped. Corfe Mullen, like Alderholt, is an example of a village whose centre of gravity has shifted with more recent development.

DURWESTON. A pony trap outside the parish church of St Nicholas in 1910 on the lane leading to Bryanston, then the home of Lord Portman. The church was completely rebuilt 40 or so years before Thomas Nesbitt took this photograph, and only the tower and porch of the medieval building survive.

Above: EAST ORCHARD. Here is the *Western Gazette* of August 1st 1899. 'TEMPERANCE FESTIVAL. The annual outdoor festival in connection with Compton Abbas, East Orchard, Fontmell, Hinton St Mary, Manston, Shroton, Stourpaine, and Sturminster Newton branches of the C.E.T.S. [Church of England Temperance Society] in one of Mr Meaders fields at Hartgrove Farm was a pleasing success. The members were conveyed to the field in waggons, brakes etc. The weather favoured the day's proceedings which commenced with a service conducted by Rev Brucke of Compton. Tea succeeded, each providing its own. A programme of sports was contested. A platform meeting was held under the chairmanship of Rev E Chappell. An address was delivered by Rev Braithwaite of Andover who deprecated the drinking of alcoholic liquor and instanced evil effects of the practice. Dancing was afterwards indulged in to the strains of Stourpaine brass band.'

Below: FRAMPTON. Holy Trinity Catholic Church, Dorchester, parish outing to Frampton Park in 1907.

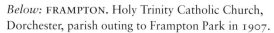

Left: HINTON MARTELL. St Joseph's Cottage Home and Chapel shortly after it was opened in 1903 by Father Alban Henry Baverstock. A place where 'little boys from bad homes could enjoy the advantages of a real home life', it housed up to 14 boys between the ages of 5 and 14. St Joseph's was one of a dozen or so Anglo-Catholic Holy Family Homes. In 1909 St Crispin's Home was established in Bournemouth as a 'continuation home' to which older boys could be transferred and taught a trade. Both homes are thought to have closed in the 1930s.

St. Joseph's Cottage and Chapel, Hinton Martel.

The Congregational Church, Longham.

T.K. Sutton
Longham.

LONGHAM. Dissenters in the area had initially met in a cottage, then a small chapel. The appointment of Joseph Notting as minister in 1839 increased the congregation, leading to the chapel's replacement with a larger building, which opened for worship in 1841. At the time it was thought that Longham was to be developed as a 'model' village. To quote from the church's excellent website: 'The New England influence is believed to come from a member of the Kemp family in the village who had visited America and is thought to have made donations towards the cost of the building. Joseph Notting was 67 years old when he died in 1863 and he is buried in the graveyard next to his beloved chapel.' The Listed Building united with the Presbyterian Church in 1972 and is now the United Reformed Church. The oak tree and small triangle of grass are now tarmac on a busy junction, whilst the short-lived Silver Star Coffee Tavern on the left is currently a bicycle shop.

LYDLINCH. One of the Reverend Samuel and Mrs Maud Hooper's summer concert parties at the Rectory in Holebrook Lane in about 1905. Alas, we have been unable to find out anything else about the concerts. In Lydlinch church is a memorial window to the Hooper's fourth and youngest son Leonard, who was killed on the Somme 12 days before his 22nd birthday in 1916 whilst serving with the Dorsetshire Regiment. The rectory still stands, though without its tower and glass-roofed verandah.

Right: MARNHULL. The Wesleyan Chapel in New Street, shortly after its completion in 1904. Methodism reached the village thanks to William Lewis (born 1799), a woolstapler, who first held services in his thatched woolcombing shed. In the 1830s a chapel was built on the site, with a gallery for musicians to play during services, and this in turn was replaced by the chapel in the photograph, now a private house, 'Providence Place'.

Below: MELBURY ABBAS. The United Temperance Fete at Cannfield Park in 1910. The photograph was taken outside the rectory (sold by the Church Commissioners in 1966). The Temperance Movement had a strong hold on the area round Shaftesbury, and both the Glyn Arms at Compton Abbas and Spreadeagle Inn at Melbury Abbas were temperance houses (see pages 117 and 121).

POXWELL. A small medieval church once stood alongside the 17th century manor house. In 1868 the owner of the house, John Trenchard, demolished the existing church and built the one in the photograph some 70 yards to the east. By the 1960s the building was in danger of collapsing and the congregation had dwindled to two. It was demolished in 1969, and only the low enclosing wall shown in the photograph survives.

PUDDLETOWN. A pair of horse-drawn Church Army vans parked in The Square in about 1900. The Church Army was founded in 1882 by the evangelist Rev Wilson Carlisle and a group of soldiers and working men and women. It held open air services, initially in the urban slums, preached by laymen and women, as a way of encouraging people to worship and read the scriptures. It continues its work to this day in 15 countries under the presidency of the former Archbishop of Canterbury, Rowan Williams. The building on the right housed the village shop.

SPETISBURY. This rare postcard shows nuns working in the garden at Spetisbury House, or St Monica's Priory, probably shortly before the First World War. From about 1800 until its demolition in 1926 the house was occupied by a succession of religious orders, refugees from religious persecution on mainland Europe. From 1907 it was the home of a community of Ursuline nuns from Normandy, exiled by a French law forbidding religious orders to teach. The 1911 census lists 34 nuns. Once established, they started a school. The building was dark and gloomy, the regime strict. The boarders were allowed one weekly bath: a nun undressed each girl down to her vest, then shut her eyes and handed her an open gown to wear in the bath. An ink blot on a letter home led to the letter being read out by a nun then pinned on the offending girl's back for all to read.

Following its closure in 1926, the buildings were bought by Walter Rigler, a Boscombe speculator, for £2,000, who a year later sold it to Thomas Oakley, a contractor, who immediately embarked on its demolition. The contents were advertised in *The Western Gazette*, including 100 pine panel doors, 16,000 roofing tiles and 200,000 clean bricks. The once overgrown Burial Ground was excluded from the sale, and in 1977 was restored and turned into a Village Garden incorporating the gravestones of the nuns and monks who had died. The site itself is occupied by housing. One of Dorset's best websites gives a much fuller history by Sue Stead of a now lost building: http://sites.google.com/site/stmonicaspriory.

SYDLING ST NICHOLAS. Looking north along Sydling Brook towards the Congregational Chapel at Downs End. Congregationalism flourished in west Dorset from the mid 18th century, with meetings in village houses and cottages. In 1834 the congregation was forced to move from its first meeting house, which was converted into a school, and a new chapel was built on a site given by Samuel Devenish, the minister. It opened in 1837, with seats for 160. When this photograph was taken in about 1880 John Thomas Smith was the minister at both Sydling and Cerne Abbas, preaching three times on Sundays and running a large adult Bible Class. Writing many years later, a Mrs Bushrod recalled that the singing 'could be heard right down the village'. The last service was held in 1969, which two people attended, and the chapel is now a private house. The barn on the left has been demolished.

WEST STAFFORD. The parish church of St Andrew is largely Jacobean of 1640, but like so many Dorset churches it fell victim to the Victorian love of 'improvement', who within a few years of this photograph added a chancel and new stained glass. For many, its principal association is as the setting for Tess's ill-fated marriage to Angel Clare in *Tess of the d'Urbervilles*. The stable on the immediate left has since been demolished, though the bend in the road remains as narrow as ever: no child with her hoop would risk standing in its centre today.

Top: WIMBORNE ST GILES. The church was built in 1742 to a design by the Bastard Brothers of Blandford, and was 'Gothicised' in the late 19th century by the architect G.F. Bodley as a memorial to the late 8th Earl of Shaftesbury, who committed suicide six months after inheriting the title, by his widow Harriet. On September 30th 1908 soldering work set the roof alight. 'A photo of our dear old church,' wrote the writer of this card, 'burned out with fire a month ago. All our bells destroyed and church burned clean out. The 9th Earl commissioned a pupil of Bodley's, the architect Ninian Comper, to undertake the restoration of the gutted and roofless building. By extending it, widening the north aisle and adding a Lady Chapel, Comper grafted High Victorianism onto Georgian spaciousness, creating a parish church that is unlike any other in Dorset. The postcard shows masons cutting new capitals and other stonework in the nave during the restoration.

Left: WINTERBORNE KINGSTON. The Wesleyan Chapel in Church Street in 1905. It opened in 1872 and is now a private house.

Bottom: WINTERBORNE STICKLAND. The Wesleyan Chapel was built in 1877 to house a growing congregation. The tall girl is holding an iron hoop, usually made by the village blacksmith, which were trundled along by a stick and were popular with both boys and girls. The thatched buildings on the right in this photograph of 1904 were destroyed by fire fifty years later.

THE VILLAGE SHOP

FONTMELL MAGNA. Although the hamlet of Bedchester was in decline by the date of this 1907 photograph it still merited a Wesleyan Chapel and its own small grocery and post office. James Hart was the postmaster, and the post arrived daily from Shaftesbury at 7.45 a.m. Both chapel and shop still stand.

LILIAN BOND's celebrated portrait of Tyneham, *Tyneham, A Lost Heritage*, gives an evocative account of the post office and shop at the turn of the 20th century:

'The premises were tiny and one five-foot counter served both shop and post office, but every inch of window space and walls was crammed with wares, the heavier articles, such as boxes of lard and bags of flour and soda, standing on the floor.

Three customers at a time produced a traffic jam and, when the counter was piled high with parcels waiting for the postman, the postmistress was scarcely visible behind the rampart.

The shop had a fine rich blend of smells, bacon and cheese predominating, with alluring under-currents of tea, liquorice and peppermint. There was a varied choice of biscuits to be had at popular prices, and chocolate and sweets to suit all comers. Fry's chocolate cream was on sale in big, thick bars at a penny apiece and a penn'orth of sugared almonds, bulls' eyes, acid drops, fruit jellies and the like filled a sizeable bag. There were comfits, too, in different shapes and colours, bearing romantic legends: – "Will you be my sweetheart?" "I Love you", "Will you be mine?" . . . and jars full of mammoth peppermint humbugs. Ha'porths were served just as willingly as the larger amounts, and a fat bag of popcorn was sold for a farthing. In fact, a penny spelt riches when spent at the shop.

A big cardboard box displayed needles and thimbles, cotton reels, mending wool, buttons and tape, all priced at a copper or two. Another box held sundry stationery items, penny bottles of ink, double sheets of glossy white notepaper pleasant to write on, pens, pencils, sealing-wax, wrappers and gum.

Shoe laces, matches, lozenges, garden seeds and balls of string, oil, candles, blacking and vinegar crowded the corners.'

Hardy was less enthusiastic, regarding the stock-in-trade of the village shop was consisting of a litle more than a 'couple of loaves, a pound of candles, a bottle of brandy-balls and lumps of delight, three or four scrubbing brushes, and a frying pan.'

But whichever description is the more accurate, the shop is always fondly remembered in almost every account of Dorset village life. Sadly, I use the past tense, because all too many have fallen victim to the arrival of the supermarket and are now private houses called 'The Old Shop' or 'The Old Post Office', some still with the bow windows of the original shop front and a letterbox let in the wall.

Every village could be relied on for a bakery, butcher's shop and dairy. In Holnest milk was sold by dairymen taking round a churn in a cart, which was measured into jugs with a ladle. In Stour Provost children took the empty milk can to the dairy in the evening, collecting it full in the morning. The Puddletown cowstalls of the Daw family enabled milk to be delivered on foot every morning from a pair of yoked buckets.

Most village shops were a crowded mixture of grocery, haberdashery and hardware store. Glady's Spriggs in Sydling St Nicholas prided herself on doing business with 60 different firms. Everything else was bought locally on market day. There were also itinerant pedlars, the Victorian equivalent of the door-to-door salesman. John Cox walked the area round Holnest with tea and draperies on his back, calling on every household and bleeding calves to prevent quarter-evil as he went, eventually setting sufficient aside to build himself a house called 'Tinker's End'. Mr Wilcox from Long Burton exchanged groceries for rabbit and moleskins. Cottagers in the south Winterborne valley grew used to the weekly visit of Freddie Chapman, almost a tramp, who walked twenty miles a day selling boot polish and laces.

Opposite page top: BERE REGIS. Now a backwater, North Street was once much busier, and both it and West Street were collectively known as 'The Street'. On the right, now a private house called 'The Corner Store' was a clothes shop, with what look like leather aprons hanging outside.

Opposite page bottom: BROADMAYNE. B & J Snook's delivery cart outside Broadmayne Stores in 1903. The shop was both grocer and bakery, 'from which the smell of newly baked bread wafted up Main Street every morning'. Better known as the Old Bakery, some villagers used to take their Christmas lunch to be roasted in its ovens. It finally closed in 1985 when it failed to meet modern regulations, and the site is now occupied by a private house.

Bere Regis.

Hills & Rowneys Series.

BROADMAYNE

CHILD OKEFORD. Two 'lost' shops. The upper photograph is of the Child Okeford and Iwerne Minster Co-Operative Stores near the junction of Upper Street and The Hollow. Before opening as a shop in 1883 it was a coffee tavern and is now Bartley House. The lower photograph is of the High Street post office in about 1900, which has only recently closed, with the postal facilities moving to the Cross Stores. The man in the suit was the postmaster/shopkeeper William Diffey.

Above: COLEHILL. Harry Newman standing in the doorway of The Stores, the village shop and post office in 1908, looking west along Smugglers Lane towards Furzehill. The Stores opened in 1897, when Frank Barrett moved his bakery a few yards to the cross roads. Frank remained both shopkeeper and postmaster until the early 1940s, to be succeeded by his daughter Amy. Colehill became a civil parish in 1894, emphasising its 19th century transformation from a scattering of thatched cottages and smallholdings into a proper community, largely composed of domestic servants and tradesmen employed by an influx of wealthier families whose brick-built houses stood amongst the pine woods.

Above: CRANBORNE. A view down Salisbury Street towards Prismalls Brothers corn store and warehouse. Their shop was on the corner, combining a grocery and bakery with the selling of patent medicines. It later became the Beehive Stores and closed in the 1980s. Both it and Budden's Ironmongery in the foreground are now private houses, as is the corn storn, now 'The Old Granary'.

Below: EVERSHOT. A cart unloading supplies outside Bird & Sons General Stores in the High Street. Remarkably, this is still the village store and both bay windows survive. Only the building on the left has been demolished, creating an entrance to what is now a car park.

GUSSAGE ALL SAINTS. The village shop in 1914. 'This is our one shop,' wrote the writer of the card on August 21, going on to say that the men 'have nearly all gone to the war.' The shop was run by the Reeks family, with a bakery on the premises, and is now a private house. In *The Gussages Past and Present* (1983) the shop is described as 'a real Aladdins Cave, you could buy anything and everything. Bread and cakes baked on the premises, groceries, clothes, medicines and animal foods.' Despite its size, the village then supported a post office, tailor, butcher, insurance and newsagent, beer shop, and carrier. Such amenities carried little weight with Sir Frederick Treves, who in 1906 thought it contained 'some of the most ancient and primitive thatched cottages to be found in Dorset.'

Above: HALSTOCK. The Triangle in about 1880, with Mary Miller's shop and post office (now a private house). The tree shown has been replaced by another, but the Triangle remains. All life is here, from the bowler-hatted roguish looking labourer on the right to the foppish young man driving the trap on the left.

HINTON MARTELL. The village shop and post office in about 1900, with the school (now the Village Hall) just visible on the right. The sub-postmistress, Mrs George Parsons, stands by the fence, whilst the two horses enjoy a nosebag of oats before returning to Ringwood. Apart from the ivy, the cottage remains unchanged, retaining the tiled porch and its timber finials on the roof.

IWERNE MINSTER. In 1908 Lord Wolverton sold the Iwerne estate to James Ismay of the White Star Shipping Line (owners of the ill-fated *Titanic*). Ismay transformed his new fiefdom into an Edwardian model village. The girls were given red cloaks, the boys blue trousers – which he insisted be worn. The cottages were provided with red blinds, a handful of which are still hanging. He built a model dairy, bacon factory, and butcher's shop– and the co-operative store in this photograph (note the millinery showroom upstairs). It remains open as Iwerne Stores to this day.

Below: LITTON CHENEY. White Cross Bakery on the road to Burton Bradstock, with the White Horse Inn the background.

The bakery was started by Maria Bligdon in the 1850s, then a domestic servant and the young wife of a village boot and shoe maker. It quickly prospered, at one point employing the creator of the Dorset Knob biscuit, Mr Moores. In due course it changed hands, and by the date of this photograph it was being run by Edwin King. Notice the 'Hovis' sign on the rear of his cart, an indication that commercial bakeries baking a standard loaf were beginning to make inroads into the popularity of the village baker. Hovis was first baked in Macclesfield in 1887, and in due course the wheat-germ enriched flour and branded baking tins were sold to other bakers. The pub fell victim to fire in 1926, and was rebuilt – and still remains open.

White Cross Bakery, Litton Cheney.

Above: MAIDEN NEWTON. The centre of the village in about 1910. Remarkably, two of the three shops visible in the photograph remain open; Tuffins as the Village Stores, whilst James Vaisey's stationers on the left is still a newsagent and stationers. Note the hangings in Tuffin's windows to keep out the heat. The stump of the village cross has been moved to the pavement on the right, and the Royal George Inn is now a private house and a restaurant.

Below: MORETON. Moreton Stores and post office began life as a simple thatched cottage on the little lane leading down to the ford over the Frome. Gradually, various architectural flourishes transformed it in this delightful if eccentric muddle of eaves, decorative brickwork – complete with clock and oriel window. It still stands, if empty, and without the clock.

Below: ORGANFORD. To this day Organford remains a tiny scattered hamlet adjoining the Sherford River just off the A35 near Lytchett Minster. Here Thomas Palmer stands outside the village shop shortly after he and his wife Selina had it built in 1894. Thomas's granddaughter, June King, has written a fine account of both Lytchett and Organford in *Memories of a Dorset Parish, Bygone Lytchett Minster*. Their first home was a pair of old cottages, where Thomas opened a bakery and Selina ran a shop in the front room. Hard work brought success. By the date of the photograph they had the grocery, a bakehouse, storage and cart sheds, and pigsties. The family finally sold the business in the 1950s, and it closed in 1998. Today it is run as a Bed and Breakfast, aptly called The Old Post Office.

OWERMOIGNE. John Westmacott outside the post office and village on the Moreton Road in 1906, which initially opened in the 1860s and continued to be run by the family until well into the 1950s. Two sons were killed in the First World War,

and a daughter went on to become the village schoolmistress. The school has long been closed, the shop in the photograph is now a private house: a later shop on a different site finally closed its doors in 2009.

SPETISBURY. Robert Hunt's 'wholesale & family grocer, provision factor, draper, outfitter & post office, The People's Supply Stores' in 1890, when it already been open for 40 years and employed two men, an errand boy to do the local deliveries, and an apprentice. It closed in the 1990s and is now a private house (see also page 63).

STOKE ABBOTT. Children lined up outside the village shop at the foot of Norway Lane in about 1895. Shortly after this photograph was taken the shop and post office moved to Holly House, and the building became a bakery run by a member of the Moore family (of Dorset Knob biscuits). The village's first postmaster in Holly House was the village blacksmith and wheelright, George Woolmington, whose daughter Evelyn took his place behind the counter, between them serving successive generations of customers until Evelyn's retirement in 1966, a total of well over 60 years. The post office/shop closed in about 1980.

Left: STOURPAINE. The upper photograph shows the village shop and post office in about 1890. The cottages on the right have all been demolished, probably when the A352 was widened. The shop closed in 2010, reopening a year later in the last building on the left, the White Horse Inn. Its renaissance owes much to 'The Pub is the Hub' scheme, initiated by the Prince of Wales, as a way of providing essential services within rural pubs.

The lower photograph is of the High Street Bakery and post office before the First World War. Although no longer the post office, the building remains a shop. Brick-built and Victorian, it probably dates to shortly before the photograph, evidence of the village's centre of gravity shifting from its medieval centre round the church to the Shaftesbury/Blandford road (A350).

Right: STOUR PROVOST. William Maidment's delivery cart outside his shop in 1895, now a private house.

Below: STOURTON CAUNDLE. The village shop and post office at the top of Golden Hill, now a private house. Philip Knott's *Book of Stourton Caundle* (2001) describes it as comprising three rooms, with the grocery on the right, a store at the back for such things as barrels of malt vinegar, and the post office just inside the entrance. Note the shoes and boots for sale in the display case to the left of the door. The shop moved in the 1950s to the bakehouse opposite, finally closing in 1991.

Below: THREE LEGGED CROSS. When this photograph was taken in 1900 the shopkeeper was Walter Stickland, whose family also owned the Traveller's Rest, here shown on the left. The turning on the right was to Verwood, whilst in the distance the lane rises over the railway bridge towards Horton. The shop later became Gregory's Store and Post Office, only to be finally demolished after further changes of ownership in 1983 and replaced by flats.

TRENT. The post office and village shop in about 1900, only a few years after Trent's transfer from Somerset to Dorset in 1896 (other neighbouring parishes transferred at the same time were Goathill, Poynington and Sandford Orcas). The principal reason for the boundary change was that all four parishes sent their poor to a Dorset workhouse, the Sherborne Union. Telegrams and postal orders were then dealt with at Nether Compton, reached by a footpath over the fields. The post office/shop later moved to another cottage, but both are now private houses.

Below: TURNWORTH. The small Dorset village was really no more than a hamlet with a population of about 140, yet it still boasted a village stores and post office. The delivery cart belonged to Alfred Dean, a Blandford butcher. The post office was run by Mrs Louisa Bolt, 'Granny' Bolt, its postmistress from 1893 to 1927, finally closing in 1946. The marriage of brick and flint is a hallmark of Turnworth's Victorian farm buildings and cottages, the estate belonging to the Parry-Okeden family, and tenanted by John Tory (on the horse).

Successive generations of Torys have been much involved in the agricultural life of the county, once farming 6,000 acres. Rider Haggard was John Tory's guest when travelling round Dorset in 1902 to report on the state of farming: 'This gentleman belongs to the old school of yeoman farmers, of whom he is the perfect type. As I looked at him, surrounded by his stalwart sons and handsome daughters, I could not help wondering whether in another score of years rural England would have many such families to show.'

FARMING THE LAND

CORFE CASTLE. Gathering hay in about 1910.

A TRAVELLER CROSSING DORSET in the mid-19th century would have seen a pattern of farming whose essentials seemed impervious to change. The central chalk downland was dominated by its flocks of sheep, the 'Golden Hoof'. First fattened on the early grass in the water meadows, they then grazed the open downland. At night they were folded over turnips and swedes in hurdle pens, 'walking dung carts' that manured the poor arable soils of the downs. 'For their dung serves the corn ground/And the wool clothes the poor,' went one Dorset song. After shearing, they were packed off back to the downs to nibble its short nutrient-rich turf.

The vale farms of Blackmore and Marshwood, with their well-watered heavy clays, produced some of the best grassland in Britain. Dorset butter was famous, as within its borders was its skimmed milk Blue Vinny cheese (it had few admirers elsewhere, one writer calling it 'more fitting to be used as barrow-wheels than for food.'). One unusual characteristic of Dorset dairying was the hiring out of cattle to a specialist dairyman at a fixed price per cow, depending on the quality of both animal and land. This gave the farmer a guaranteed income, spared him the worry of managing a herd, whilst offering the dairyman and his family an incentive to improve the yield of the cows in their care and the chance to become independent farmers in their own right.

Elsewhere in the county flax and hemp were grown in the west, principally to supply the local sail-cloth and rope-making industries. The sandy heathlands in the east were the poorest, though as Bournemouth grew and fertilisers became available they were readily adapted for horticulture. Despite its stony uplands, Purbeck's farms echoed those of the downland, with their fields extending up the valley sides. Altogether, in 1873 the average size of the county's 5,420 farms was 86 acres (a century later, in 1979, the number of farms had halved and their acreage doubled).

In 1899 a project to provide county by county histories of England was started. Originally dedicated to Queen Victoria, and still being published today, it was called the *Victoria History of the Counties of England*. The title alone suggests the dry scholarly fact-based content. But here is an excerpt from the opening paragraph of the chapter of agriculture in the 1908 volume on Dorset: 'the lot of the agriculturist, bright as were its prospects in the earlier years, is now cast in very hard places. Indeed, so great has been the change that the farmer of 1800, were he alive now, would scarcely recognize his county.'

Sheep were the hardest hit. Flock totals fell from 500,000 to 300,000 in the five years following 1895, which in turn led to the sluices controlling the water meadows becoming abandoned. Flax and hemp cultivation virtually ceased. The arable that had once provided the corn for Dorset's mills became poor-quality permanent pasture. Altogether 20% of all Dorset's farmers gave up the struggle between 1875 and 1902, whilst the reduction in labourers was even greater.

But it wasn't all gloom. The dairy farmers of the Blackmore and Marshwood Vales proved the most resilient. In 1906 5 million gallons of liquid milk went from Dorset to London by rail. More travelled north to the Midlands and to factories making a standardised Cheddar cheese. The loss of the traditional yeoman farmer, the 'three bottle man' (most of it port), was balanced by the rise of the tenant farmer, 'who by dint of early rising and late retiring, and by constant supervision and close application to his work, manages to snatch a hard-earned livelihood from the land.'

Two far-sighted pioneers also did what they could to stem the tide. In 1880 Sir Robert Edgcumbe bought 343 acres at Martinstown for smallholdings, which he divided into 80 lots of between one and nine acres. The land was sold cheaply, 10% on purchase, the balance over nine years. The 27 new owners included farm labourers, stonemasons, a policeman, postman, blacksmith and shopkeeper – all of whom paid off the balance well before it was due. Alfred Dwight was a gardener for Lord Ilchester at Abbotsbury, his wife a lady's maid. Using their savings to buy a plot, they sowed flowers, rising at dawn to sell them fresh in Dorchester. Soon tomatoes and cucumbers filled their new greenhouses, then their South Street shop. A farm that had once supported 21 people ultimately provided a living for 100 smallholders and their families. Land, believed Sir Robert Edgcumbe, was 'for growing men and women', not just food.

In 1914, the owner of the London department store bearing his name, Ernest Debenham, began the purchase of what eventually became the 10,000 acre Bladen Estate, centred on Briantspuddle. His intention was to combine self-sufficiency with rural employment and good farming practise by selling the estate's produce straight from the farm, a then novel idea. Work was delayed by the outbreak of the First World War, but at its height the estate's dairy herds were producing 20,000 gallons of milk a day, much of it sold in wax coated cartons. In 1931 Debenham was knighted for his services to agriculture and his pioneering approach to farming helped sow the seeds for the formation of the Soil Association in 1946.

Above: AFFPUDDLE MILL. The original mill on the River Piddle was mentioned in the Domesday Book, passing from the Abbots of Cerne into secular ownership after the Dissolution of the Monasteries. By the later 19th century it belonged to the Frampton family, who lived at Moreton, and the Estate Diary for 1895 notes that the old house alongside the mill 'is quite gone to pieces'. A new house was built to replace it at a cost of £350 by a Mr Davies of Dorchester. The following year a new iron waterwheel was fitted, and in 1903 a steam oven was fitted for the then tenant, Mr C W Billey, who combined miller and baker and which is probably when this photograph was taken. The mill wheel stopped turning in 1923 – though much of the machinery survived into the 1960s.

Below: ASHMORE. Gathering hazel nuts in about 1880. In a 1953 booklet about Sixpenny Handley intended for the village children to learn a little about the life of their grandparents, Mr F. Adams wrote: 'After the harvest came nutting in the woods. This was the women's job chiefly, but the woodmen and hurdle makers joined in too. During a good season hundreds of sacks of nuts were sent to the London market. In some seasons a considerable sum of money was earned in this way. One villager, when 84, told me that as a young man he could earn as much as £1 a day. He had three brothers and together with his parents the total income of this one family could be £4-5 a day for 3 or 4 weeks.' And that was at a time when the agricultural wage was 11/- a week.

Above: ASHMORE. Watering sheep in the pond, with Bay Cottage in the background and the village school and its playground just visible on the left.

Below: BERE REGIS. The first commercial watercress beds in Dorset were planted in 1892 when William Bedford discovered natural springs south of the village at Doddings. In due course other local beds were established in the Bere Stream's calcium and nutrient rich waters. In the early days it was largely a winter crop, providing seasonal employment for men in the beds, cutting and pulling, and women in the packing sheds. By 1920 the company was known as Bedford and Jesty, four years later becoming the first firm to coin a brand name for a vegetable product, 'Sylvasprings'. By then it was the largest producer of watercress in the country, cutting 3,500 cwt a year, much of which was eaten in the Midlands and North. The beds are still harvested, and are part of Vitacress.

Above: BLOXWORTH, Stevens Farm. The early 17th century farm cottage and range of farm buildings comprised the smallest of the four farms on the 3,765 acre Bloxworth Estate, which had belonged to the Pickard-Cambridge family since 1751. In 1900, following the death of Jocelyn Pickard-Cambridge, the estate was inherited by his daughter Mary, who promptly returned from Sri Lanka, where her husband Frederick Lane was a tea planter. Stevens Farm was then tenanted by George Breen, who eventually emigrated to Canada when the smaller farms were amalgamated – a common practise after the First World War and through the years of depression that followed. Two of Mary and Frederick's sons were killed in the First World War, and the estate was sold after the death of a third, Ernest, in 1958 – two centuries after it had first been bought.

Below: BLOXWORTH. George Young was the manager of the Home Farm on the estate, and this photograph was probably taken at the same time as that of the pigs at Barford Farm (see page 106). Dorset claims three breeds of sheep, the now rare Portland, and the Dorset Horn and Dorset Down. The Down originated in the early 1800s as a crossing of local Hampshire and Wiltshire ewes with Southdown rams. Its principal merits are hardy ewes able to withstand the downland weather and early maturing lambs. All three Dorset breed numbers fell dramatically as a result of the agricultural depression, never really recovering. In 2000 there were altogether fewer Dorset Downs in the county than in this one photograph, but a pedigree prize-winning flock is kept by David and Ruth Wilkins at Rampisham Hill Farm (see www.rampishamhillfarm.co.uk).

Churchill, Photo.,   FLOCK OF 1,750 DOWN EWES AND LAMBS   *Wareham.*
(the property of G. T. Young, Bloxworth).

Above: BRADFORD PEVERELL. Giles Cross and the junction with Tilly Whim and Gascoyne lanes, with what is now Gascoyne New Barn on the right. 'How do you like this photo of our busy country?' wrote the author of this 1910 card. The thatch has gone, and the open cartshed become a garage, but little else has changed in this view looking west towards the village. This whole area was redeveloped by Hastings Nathaniel Middleton, who inherited the manor in 1848. Middleton rebuilt the lane, as well as stables, a granary, a piggery and a calves' house. The two cottages in the photograph were built in 1871 at a cost of £231, which were then let to a farmer who in turn sublet them to his workers.

Below: BRIANTSPUDDLE, The Dairy Ring. The village was the centrepiece of Ernest Debenham's 10,000 acre Bladen Estate. When work finally got underway after the First World War Debenham's links with the Arts & Crafts movement defined the architecture of the new buildings, from the cottages to the poultry farm, grain silos to transport yard. This photograph is of the central diary, with the cheese room with its tower in the centre and the herdsman's house on the right. The entire estate has gradually been sold. The Central Dairy became derelict and in the 1990s was converted to housing.

VILLAGE STORES.
SERIES I.

BLADEN DAIRIES.

THRESHING AT CHETNOLE.

Top: BRYANSTON. 'Some of Lord Portman's Prize Cattle', 1911. The herd of Red Devons established by the 1st Lord Portman (1799-1888) at Bryanston was one of the most celebrated in the country, producing dams and sires whose bloodlines fostered national improvements to the breed. Politics and cows were his lordship's principal interests, and he was one of the founding fathers of the Royal Agricultural Society of England. Describing a visit to the Home Farm in 1902, Rider Haggard was awed by its splendour. 'Never before,' he wrote, 'have I seen such buildings or cottages: the very cows are provided with softer sorts of wood on which to kneel.' The bulls were all named, of which Nelson, Dignity, Vulcan, Royal Windsor are typical.

Bottom: CHETNOLE. Threshing at Manor Farm 1907. Edwin Mitchell was then its tenant, and the name of his 25 year old son Herbert Stanley can be seen on the cart on the right. After the First World War Herbert bought the 170 acre farm, one of four in the village which over the years have been amalgamated into a single holding by successive owners. Steam engines went from farm to farm, usually hauling the thresher and a sleeping van. The corn was taken from the ricks by waggon, fed into the thresher, which then separated the corn from the straw and fed the corn into sacks using power from a belt and flywheel on the steam engine.

CHISWELL, PORTLAND. Driving Portland sheep into the 'Gut', the narrow creek on the Mere, so that they could be washed prior to shearing. There were traditionally four flocks on the island, each of about 1,000, which were much used for mutton and manuring the open fields. The ewes rarely had more than one lamb, and by the 1970s the Portland was nearly extinct. Although still a rare breed, there are now 250 registered flocks in the country. The Mere has long since been built over, and is now occupied by the Weymouth & Portland National Sailing Academy, Osprey Quay and Portland Marina.

46619. CORFE CASTLE.

CORFE CASTLE. Dorset Down sheep waiting in Station Road to be put aboard a train and taken to market. The station had a cattle dock into which livestock were herded before being driven up a ramp onto trucks. It was very much two-way traffic, for the opening of the Wareham to Swanage line in 1885 was a key factor in bringing tourists to the castle. The line closed in 1972, reopening in 1995 as the Swanage Railway, and is now one of Dorset's most popular attractions.

CORFE MULLEN. The Mill, Mill Street, in about 1900. The early Victorian corn mill on the River Stour, though closed and now a guesthouse, remains a familiar landmark on the A31 and is largely unchanged.

KING'S STAG. A draper's cart outside the Blackmore Vale Dairy Company factory on Holwell Road in about 1900.

MAIDEN NEWTON. A waggon laden with corn on the Dorchester road in 1905. Its destination was the mill on the River Frome in the centre of the village, where the Swatridges were the millers. The mill closed during the First World War, and was later used for making ropes and church carpeting. The whole complex is now in private use. The barn and cottage on the left have both been demolished and new houses built on the site.

MELBURY OSMOND. Henry Saunders outside the mill at Lower Holt in about 1895. The water-driven corn mill finally stopped in 1948, and remained empty till 1975, when it was converted into a private house. Note the fine brasses on his team of horses.

Above: MILTON ABBAS. Ploughs team enjoying their 'nammet' at Luccombe Farm. A two-horse plough team could plough about 1½ acres a day; a modern tractor with a five furrow plough can do between 25 and 35.

Below: NETHER CERNE. Feeding the ducks in the late 19th century, probably when either John Meech or George Baker were the millers. The overshot wheel was built by Maggs of Bourton in 1819 and is thought to be one of the oldest iron waterwheels in the country to have survived. It remained in place until about 1950, when it was pushed from the wheel-pit into the River Cerne, only to be rescued nearly 30 years later by the Castletown Waterwheel Group, and is now on display at the Sherborne Steam and Waterwheel Centre. There is no sign of the mill buildings and adjacent cottage, all of which have been demolished.

The Mill, Nether Cerne.

OKEFORD FITZPAINE. Edward Phillips & Sons Hill View Dairies was typical of the larger dairy factories that grew up around the Blackmore Vale to take advantage of the coming of the railway, eventually employing 50 or so men and women. The Phillips were a yeoman farming family, and by 1843 Joseph Phillips was both milking at Parkmill Farm and acting as a factor for butter and cheese produced locally on other farms. By 1895 Joseph had retired to Stroud Farm, another family farm tenanted from the Pitt-Rivers Estate, who owned Okeford Fitzpaine, and Edward Phillips had given his name to the business and opened a factory off Upper Street in the middle of the village.

The first photograph shows Edward standing alongside a milk delivery cart outside the entrance to the dairy, beyond which is Pleydell's Farmhouse where he lived. The second photograph shows a general view of the dairy and butter house with a line of 17 gallon churns. and the third one cheese waiting to be loaded.

Milk was either collected or delivered early in the morning by local farmers, and then either cooled and shipped out from Shillingstone Station to Bournemouth or made into blended butter and cheese, the whey being sold to local pig farms. The cheeses were both a Cheddar and Blue Vinny, for which they won prizes.

In the 1950s the family sold the business to Malmesbury & Parsons in Bournemouth and it finally closed in 1972. The role of the Phillips family in village life is commemorated by two east windows in the church, and the legacy they provided for its upkeep and that of the churchyard. The entire factory site has been developed for housing.

OSMINGTON. Longhorn cattle outside Charity Farm, Church Lane, in 1911. More common in the far west of Dorset, the building is a longhouse dating from the 16th century, with its cattle byre and dwelling under one roof. It owes its name to being bought by the Corporation of Weymouth and Melcombe Regis with a bequest by Sir Samuel Mico, the rent paying for an annual sermon and to help 12 poor seamen. Of Osmington's six dairy farms, only one still survives. Charity Farm's grain store, cart shed and other old buildings have all been converted into private houses.

Below: PAMPHILL. Herbert Standfield was born in Milborne St Andrew in 1851 and in 1904, when this photograph was taken, was the tenant of Barford Farm, Cowgrove, on the Kingston Lacy Estate. The crossing of the Yorkshire White with the Berkshire was common amongst pig breeders at the turn of the 20th century, resulting in a pig that grew fast and fattened easily, reaching 95 kilos at 20 weeks. Dorset's most common pig was the black and white Wessex Saddleback, which originated in the New Forest as a cross between two indigenous bacon breeds. Barford Farm is today celebrated for its garden and range of ice creams.

To produce the Best Bacon in the Shortest Time, use Yorkshire Boars with Berkshire Sows, or vice versa, both may be obtained, in perfection, from the BARFORD HERDS.

A few BREEDING SOWS of the Celebrated Pedigree Large WHITE YORKSHIRE HERD of H. STANDFIELD, BARFORD FARM, WIMBORNE.

Above: PORTESHAM. A shepherd with his flock in Front Street. In 1900 working hours for farm labourers were from 6 a.m. to 6.p.m., with only Sunday free. A shepherd's wages were 13 shillings. There were two substantial farms in the village, Portesham (600 acres) and Manor Farm (900 acres), who between them employed 52 men. Farms of similar size today might employ two.

Centre: SHILLINGSTONE. The chalk pit on Okeford Hill, seen here from Sandy Lane, became the site of the Shillingstone Lime and Stone Company, which formed in 1924 to extract lime from the hillside. Annual production rose to 20,000 tons, with three kilns producing quicklime for spreading on farmland and for builders' merchants. During the First World War moss was gathered from Okeford Hill for use as a medical dressing.

Bottom: SHILLINGSTONE. The aptly-named miller, Frederick Miller, outside Bere Marsh Mill in 1885, when there were 120 mills still working in the county. Bere Marsh Mill closed in 1923, and the only surviving traces are the ruins of the dam and some footings. There were once 20 mills on the River Stour, and though most milled corn or animal feed they included weaving and cloth fulling mills.

THE DAIRY, STUDLAND.

Above: STUDLAND. The Dairy House, which at the turn of the 20th century was the home of a dairyman, J. Honeybun, his wife and five children. On August 8th 1908 three of the children woke to find their cottage on fire, due to a beam catching alight behind the washroom copper. Swanage Fire Brigade soon arrived, but the water supply was only sufficient to dampen down the adjoining cottages and the Dairy House was destroyed. Although local campers helped the Honeybuns salvage what they could, a subscription list was started to help the family replace the furniture and clothing lost in the fire. Henrietta Bankes, the sole owner of the Bankes Estate following the death of her husband, paid for the Dairy House to be rebuilt, and for a while it became a tea room.

Below left: STURMINSTER MARSHALL. This view of the High Street from Kents Lane railway bridge in about 1900 hints at what was once one of the county's largest and most successful enterprises – the Bailey Gate Milk Factory. It began life in 1888 after Henry Tory, a local farmer, realised that the arrival of the railway and the accelerating growth of Bournemouth (5,896 in 1871, 37, 650 in 1891) provided a new market for fresh milk from the surrounding dairy farms. The milk was despatched in churns from a loading bay at the station, and here a farmer can be seen about to turn in towards the station yard. Under Henry's son Clement butter and cheese rooms were built, as well as a coal yard, animal feed mill and piggery. In 1905, the family sold what was now Bailey Gate Diaries to Carters of Boscombe, who in turn were taken over by United Dairies ten years later. By the outbreak of the Second World War it had become the largest cheese producer in Europe, importing 50,000 gallons of milk a day from as far west as Carmarthen and exporting 20 tons of cheese. The surplus whey was separated and dried for animal feed. By the mid-1950s it had nearly 300 employees. The closure of the Somerset and Dorset Railway in 1966 was the first nail in the coffin, though the factory remained open until 1978. As with the railway station, its site is now occupied by Bailie Gate Industrial Estate.

Above: TARRANT KEYNESTON. Watering farm horses. The small bridge over the River Tarrant has since been replaced, and the chapel on the right is now a private house.

Below: THORNCOMBE. Some of the 60 sheep struck dead by lightning on June 18th 1914. It was an omen of a much great tragedy. Ten days later the Archduke Franz Ferdinand and his wife were assassinated in Sarajevo, sparking off a chain of events that led to the outbreak of the First World War in early August. The one redeeming virtue in this photograph is the fine display of woven hazel hurdles.

Baltington Farm House, Tyneham.

HOME FARM, TYNEHAM.

TYNEHAM. 1908 photographs of the two farmhouses, Baltington and Home Farm. The Hull family tenanted both farms for many years, James at Baltington, his brother Joseph at Home Farm. Both buildings lie within the army ranges and are now derelict. Tyneham was virtually self-sufficient, with poultry, two dairies, a piggery, a flock of Dorset Down sheep, half a dozen working horses, and enough arable land to fill the granary and provide winter fodder for the livestock. The building to the right of Home Farm was the dairy house, whose upper floor Lilian Bond remembered as 'all one airy room whose well-scrubbed boards were covered with rows of big blue vinny cheeses, in different stages of the ripening process.'

Top: UPWEY. The four storey 1802 mill alongside Church Street. The wheel is unusual in that it is fed from two sides at different levels: one side from a leat, the other via a stream from the River Wey.

Centre: WAREHAM ST MARTIN. Cutting furze (gorse) on Keysworth Farm in February 1907 with an 'Admiral' mower. The Pain family farmed the marginal land between the Wareham to Poole railway line and the edge of Poole Harbour. Furze was traditionally used by bakeries for their bread ovens. It quickly raised the oven temperature, leaving little ash for raking out. Elsewhere on Purbeck it had a wide variety of uses, from being packed tightly between posts to create stalls for the cattle and as a packing material for the nearby potteries in Sandford.

Below: WEST STAFFORD. Filling a water cart on the lane near Stafford House. Despite being only a few miles from Dorchester, mains water and electricity did not reach West Stafford until 1949. See also Fifehead Neville (page 48) for a similar photograph.

Above: WHITCHURCH CANONICORUM. Higher Abbott's Wootton Farm in 1905. The farm is one of five in the manor of Wootton Abbas that belonged to Abbotsbury Abbey until the Dissolution of the Monasteries in the 16th century. The long gently sloping valley running north from the River Char and Baker's Cross has been farmed since Saxon times and despite the enclosure of the common fields remains little changed. One result of enclosure was the naming of fields, often as a joke: hence a one acre plot in the valley being named 'Thousand Acres'.

Below: WINTERBORNE WHITECHURCH. Bert Maidment and Herman Cuff leading a cow on Blandford Hill outside the Methodist Chapel in about 1909. The cow belonged to Ernest Foster, a smallholder for whom they both worked part time. Herman was also the village cobbler. The iron railings on the right were removed during the Second World War and the house in the background is Bell Vue, once one of the three inns in the village, 'The Bell'.

INNS AND BREWERIES

RAMPISHAM. The Tiger's Head in 1905. The inn was rebuilt 10 years later
and finally closed in the late 1990s.

Traditionally, Dorset's country pubs played as important a role in the life of the village as its church, shop or school. They were its social centre, where men – and to a lesser extent women – gathered to gossip and exchange information. In an age without telephones, the pub was the place where news of births, courtship and illness was passed from one member of a family to the next. The economy of the agricultural year was what paid for a pint and put a wage in most pockets, and the pub was the place in which prices were discussed, the weather grumbled about, the harvest supper celebrated. The annual Club outing always ended in the pub's largest room, often with dancing to the village band followed by a hangover. A number of Dorset villages were owned by absentee landlords, whose agents annually collected cottagers' rents at a table in the pub. Before the advent of the motorcar, many were also coaching inns, providing a meal and a bed for travellers.

In 1900 there were 102,000 pubs in England and Wales, a number that had more than halved by 2013. In 1900 it was claimed that every male downed 73 gallons of beer a year, or a pint and a half a day – much of it illegally watered down with small doses of strychnine added in compensation. By the late 19th century the days of the rough and ready alehouse were over. Licenses required a magistrate's approval: both for beer and wine and spirits. Potential landlords were presumed to be of 'good character', which meant that many were retired soldiers or sailors.

Prior to the outbreak of the First World War licensing hours varied, 'according to local practise'. The Bush in Winterborne Kingston had only a 6 day license, which its landlord evaded by running a Sunday 'slate'. Dorset's oldest license is claimed by the World's End at Almer, dating to 1589. The newest in the period covered by this book were those built to serve Dorset's rural railways stations and halts. Most were thatched, many boasted only one bar, some just a counter and a few barrels of beer brewed in an outhouse.

The national reduction in breweries is even more dramatic than that of pubs: from 6,500 in 1900 to 142 by 1980. Traditionally, Dorset was dominated by four breweries, all of them in towns: Hall & Woodhouse (Blandford Forum), Devenish & Groves (Weymouth), Eldridge Pope (Dorchester), and Palmers in Bridport. But according to the 1901 census there were 263 maltsters and brewers plying their trade in the county, many of them serving a handful of pubs. The 21 pubs of the Crown Brewery in Fontmell Magna were bought by eight local breweries when it ceased brewing in 1904. Marnhull supported five malthouses and two breweries, of which the largest, Marnhull Brewery, passed through six different hands before its 36 pubs were acquired by Eldridge Pope in 1913. The lovely thatched Milton Brewery served only four pubs. Despite being only a few miles apart, both Durweston and Shroton had their own breweries.

Dorset has not been immune to the closure of pubs and well over half those open in 1900 have long since called 'last orders'. Drink/driving legislation, the ban on smoking, the sale of cheap alcohol by the supermarkets, a change in our tastes and habits – all these have played their part. Happily, in recent years the decline has steadied. Most pubs offer food. The designation of the Jurassic Coast as a UNESCO World Heritage Site has brought an ever increasing number of visitors to the county. The arrival of the micro-brewery, of which Dorset boasts a generous share, has transformed the fortunes of many pubs and immeasurably improved the quality of their beers. Some are small, like Wriggle Valley Brewery in Ryme Intrinseca, whilst its larger cousins range from the Dorset Piddle Brewery in Piddlehinton to the Isle of Purbeck Brewery in Studland.

ALMER. The World's End in about 1910. Originally called the Red Lion, it had only recently changed its name when this photograph was taken, possibly because George Dominey had just succeeded his father John as its landlord. More recently, it was rebuilt in 1991 by Hall & Woodhouse after a fire and remains one of the county's most popular pubs. General Montgomery had lunch there in 1940, an event recorded in a framed letter hanging in the bar.

Lads of the Village. 1936   Bradford Abbas.   Dorset

GEORGE CHAINEY, 89. SIDNEY PARSONS, 83. THOMAS COOMBS, 91. SAMUEL RING, 92. JAMES HIGGINS, 89.
TOTAL 444 YEARS   (ELDRIDGE, POPE & Co, Ltd.,)

BRADFORD ABBAS. The Rose & Crown. The top photograph shows staff and customers outside the pub to inspect a flooded Church Rd in about 1900. By then the Rose & Crown was the only survivor of the four inns that once served the 400 strong population. The building had once been a farmhouse with its own brewhouse, and remains open as a pub to this day. The only modern addition to this view is the War Memorial, which stands midway between the pub and the houses on the left, and bears the names of nearly 100 villagers killed in the First World War.

In 1936 British Movietone News filmed five of the regulars downing their pints in the Rose & Crown, making both pub and men famous. When the film was shown in Yeovil they were treated as film stars, posing for photographs. The five had a combined age of 444 and here are shown in 'Lads of the Village', a publicity postcard issued by the Dorchester brewers Eldridge Pope: from left to right George Chaney (89), Sidney Parsons (83), Thomas Coombs (91), Samuel Ring (92) and James Higgins (89). Of the five, Samuel Ring lived to be the oldest, dying at 96. Born in the village, he carried the Sick Benefit Club banner on Club Days and it was said he never missed a day's work in 76 years.

BROADWINDSOR. In 1910 the village suppported three inns, of which only the White Lion remains open. The top photograph is of The Cross Keys, now a private house, though the façade remains largely unchanged. The lower photograph is of The George, once a substantial coaching inn known as the Castle (closed 1960). Just visible on the cottage to its left is a plaque of 1902 commemorating the September night in 1651 when Charles II slept in it following his flight from the Battle of Worcester. Note the sign promising 'Good Accommodation for Motorists'. Mitchell, Toms & Co were a Chard brewery who closed in 1936, only a few years after this photograph was taken.

Above: CERNE ABBAS. The Red Lion Hotel, now the Giant Inn, is the only remaining free house in a village that was once famous for its beers and 14 inns. The original inn was destroyed in a fire in 1898 and rebuilt by Groves Brewery, hence the Victorian leaded windows. The two boys are sitting on the 'chute', a hole in the street that once carried drinking water from St Augustine's Well to Long Street via the town pond and the culvert in Abbey Street.

Centre: COMPTON ABBAS, WEST COMPTON. The Glyn Arms Temperance House in about 1900. In the foreground is what is now the A350 between Blandford and Shaftesbury. Much of the village was bought by the banker Sir Richard Carr Glyn in 1838, and the family remained landlords until just after the First World War, when 46 cottages and over 1,000 acres were sold. The Glyn Arms is now Glyn Farm.

Bottom: GODMANSTONE. The Smith Arms. The medieval building on the banks of the River Piddle was originally a smithy. Charles II is reputed to have stopped there on his flight from Worcester to have his horse shod and asked for a drink. On being told by the blacksmith that he had no licence, the king granted him one on the spot. The inn once had an entry in the *Guinness Book of Records* as Britain's smallest public house, and was much photographed. The bar was 11 ft 9 inches by 15 feet and the sloping ceiling 6 ft 2 inches at its highest point. The building next door was once the village shop, but both shop and pub are now closed.

GRIMSTONE. The Royal Yeoman. Now a private house on the A37 with bed and breakfast accommodation and a Caravan Club camping site in the garden. Its landlord in 1895 was Albert Pardey, who also ran the mill next door, which began life as a medieval cloth mill and closed in 1981 after making dog biscuits: it still stands empty today. The inn must surely have relied on neighbouring Frampton for custom (where inns were banned by the local squire), for although it boasted a railway station the 1881 census lists Grimstone's population of independent means as four.

HALSTOCK. The Quiet Woman in about 1910. It owes its name to the death of a unmarried local girl called Juthware, who was beheaded with an axe by her brother in the false belief that she was pregnant. According to the legend, Juthware then picked up her own head and walked silently with it to Halstock church, placing it on the altar before finally dying. Many years later her head and body were taken to Sherborne Abbey. Although the inn has closed, the house now offers family-run bed and breakfast accommodation. The card was written by 'Big Bruvver' to his sister, nicknamed 'Wippet', in Blackheath, and in part reads, 'This will give you some idea of the type of village I have to hunt out – miles from anywhere. You can't see the sign very well but her gory head is tucked under her arm – a good sample of the the brand of wit I have to put with down here.'

Below: HOLWELL. The Fox Inn, whose landlord in 1903 was Walter Fox. The inn had a chequered history. In 1883, following the death of an earlier landlady, the villagers petitioned the local magistrates to close it permanently, on the grounds that a village with a population of 417 did not require two public-houses. Of the 67 men who signed it, 19 were unable to write their names and made only a X. The villagers ultimately had their wishes, for it was eventually closed and demolished. Only its name lives on, in a nearby development of modern bungalows named Fox's Close.

Left: LYDLINCH. The Three Boars. This 1904 postcard was written and posted in Lydlinch to an address in the village. Now a private house on the A357.

Below: LYTCHETT MINSTER, Bakers Arms. Although the pub remains open and still thatched, only the road sign on the left indicates that the brick and cob building once stood on a junction linking Poole, Wareham and Dorchester. Today it sits well away from the roundabout on the main road. There was a bakery attached, hence the name, though it was originally 'St Clements Inn'. The Bakers Arm stood empty and semi-derelict for many years, but was bought and rescued by Tom Porter, and more recently has reopened after a major refurbishment.

Maiden Newton. Old White Horse and Cross.

Left: MAIDEN NEWTON. The 17th century White Horse Inn prior to its demolition by Devenish in 1898. There was widespread opposition to the demolition, led by the recently-formed Society for the Protection of Ancient Buildings, who asked Thomas Hardy to intervene in the hope that the façade could be preserved. Hardy had trained as an architect and knew the building well, but his report was pessimistic: 'the landlord's contention that no ordinary traveller likes to occupy the bedrooms as they are is obviously true.' When demolition started, the thatch was found to be 5 feet thick. Devenish built a new and remarkably unattractive White Horse inn on the site, which has since been converted into flats.

MANSTON. The Plough in about 1900. The pub's Edwardian tenants were a Mr and Mrs Courage, one of whose triplets drowned when still a child and whose ghost still plays by the fireplace.

MANSWOOD, The Drum, probably shortly after the First World War. The tiny hamlet is near Witchampton and is best known for the Buildings, 120 yards of continuous thatch incorporating 12 cottages and thought to be the longest stretch of thatch in the country. The inn has long been closed and is now a private house. Note that Bert Meaden was only licensed to sell beer and tobacco, not wine and spirits.

MARNHULL BREWERY in about 1885, seen from the corner of Carraway Lane, when it was known as Jennings, Styring & Co. The lovely bow windows in the pair of 17th century cottages (now the Old Malthouse) were put in by the brewer Thomas Burt in about 1799. The Brewery was bought by Eldridge Pope shortly before the First World War, who in turn sold it to Hall & Woodhouse in 1935. By the 1970s the brewery and its various buildings had all been sold and converted into private houses and flats, the now gabled main building remaining a local landmark.

Above: MARNHULL. Recruits for the Dorset Regiment lined up outside The Crown in 1914. Its dozen battalions saw service on the Western Front, in the Middle East and Gallipoli. A memorial to the 4,060 men of the Regiment killed in action during the First World War was unveiled in France in 2011. It stands on the start line for the Battle of the Somme, 1 July 1916, a day on which 350 soldiers from the Regiment died.

Below: MELBURY ABBAS. The Spread Eagle Inn in about 1895, with a true Dorset Waggon outside and when William Alford was its landlord. Once the Red Lion, The pub's position at the foot of the hill that shares its newer name made it a popular stopping place before the steep climb to Fontmell Down. Shortly after this photograph was taken it called 'last orders' and became a Temperance Inn, with a rifle range and a 12 acre smallholding. Today it is a private house on the busy upper road between Blandford and Shaftesbury.

OKEFORD FITZPAINE. The New Inn. The pub closed in 1960 and its skittle alley was moved to the villages's only surviving pub, the Royal Oak, which can be seen below in the 1920 photograph.

Right: OSMINGTON. The Plough Inn in 1905. The Plough belonged to Devenish, and stood on the left hand side of the road as you entered it from Weymouth. It probably opened in about 1850, but was demolished in the late 20th century. Bungalows known as Plough Cottages replaced it, but these too have now been demolished and houses built in their place.

Below: PIDDLETRENTHIDE. In 1889, which is about when this photograph was taken, the Piddle Valley village boasted five pubs (The European at White Lackington, The Sun, New Inn, Green Dragon and Five Bells), of these only two survive, both with different names. This is the Green Dragon, when David Drake was the landlord, and is now the Piddle Inn.

PUDDLETOWN (Note the spelling on the card). Ye Old Cat in 1212. The thatched pub stood on the Northbrook approach to the village. After being destroyed by fire, it was replaced by the red-brick Blue Vinny, which remains open today. Ye Old Cat's name survives in a ditty that reinforces Thomas Hardy's account of the village's reputation for hard drinking:
'Into Church
Out of Church,
Into Cat,
Out of Cat,
Into Piddle.'

The Cross, Shapwick.

Above: SHAPWICK. The Anchor Inn, with the remains of the medieval stone cross on the left. The inn owes its name to being close to what once was the highest navigable point on the River Stour. Much of Shapwick, including the Anchor, was destroyed by fire in 1881, and the pub was not rebuilt by Hall & Woodhouse until the 1920s.

Below: SHILLINGSTONE. The Old Ox Inn, which though now whitewashed remains open. Beyond it lay the New Ox, once the premises of the village undertaker, and now known as Stour House.

SHILLINGSTONE. T. NESBITT.

Above: SHROTON. The White Hart. The pub was originally owned by the short-lived Shroton Brewery (1805-1889). It burnt down in the 1920s, was rebuilt on a slightly different site and renamed The Cricketers in the 1990s.

Below: THREE LEGGED CROSS. The Travellers Rest stood on the old turnpike road between Ringwood and Cranborne at a time when the whole area was one of small market gardens. This view looks south towards Ringwood, near the turning to Verwood. In due course the pub was much modified and renamed the Woodcutters. Recently demolished, a care home now stands on the site. The Salisbury-based Gibbs Mew & Co Brewery closed in 1997.

Left: TOLLER PORCORUM. The Old Swan. In 1903 the thatched pub in the photograph was demolished and replaced by a new building, which in turn closed in 1999. Ten years later it was sold at auction by Palmers, and despite an attempt to 'Save our Swan' by the village it has since been converted into a house.

Below: TOLPUDDLE. The Crown in 1907. In the 1920s the Hall & Woodhouse pub was burnt down by sparks from a steam-powered dray as it was leaving after making a delivery – a fate suffered by the Prince of Wales in Puddletown on the same day. Both were rebuilt, though the Prince of Wales is now flats, but the Crown is still open, though it was renamed The Martyrs Inn in 1952.

Above: WHITCHURCH CANONICORUM. The Five Bells. The 18th century inn owes its name to the village church of St Candida and Holy Cross, whose tower once housed only five bells (the three that make up the present eight were installed early in the 20th century, two of them in 1912 to commemorate the coronation of George V). The thatched pub shown in the photograph burnt down on Guy Fawkes Day 1904, and was rebuilt the following year. Only the entrance flagstones survive from the original. The pub is still open and plays an important role in the life of the village.

Below: WINFRITH NEWBURGH. The Red Lion in 1914. Although no longer thatched, the pub remains open on the A352 near the turning to the village. Note the footbridge over the little River Win and the postman. A car is parked to the left of Wright's grocery cart , a sure sign of changing times.

Above: WINTERBOURNE ABBAS. The Coach and Horses, probably shortly after the First World War. The pub has recently closed. The last pint brewed at Weymouth's Devenish Brewery was in 1985, and the whole site has since been redeveloped.

Below: WINTERBORNE KINGSTON. The Bush in 1895, when William Jeans was its landlord. It finally closed in 1965 and is now a private house, the Old Bush.

FIELD SPORTS

LORD PORTMAN'S HOUNDS. The card is postmarked 1911, and was sent to a Miss Lucy Keen in Southampton. On the back is written, '(1) The Whip, (2) Mr Jones – the Huntsman, (3) The Honourable Lascelles. Lord Portman's Kennels are only two minutes from Blandford and are often over this way.'

WHATEVER WE MAY THINK of the rights and wrongs of foxhunting today, in 19th century Dorset no other sport matched its popularity or importance. 'The rural population generally incline to a hunt,' wrote Surtees in *Mr Sponge's Sporting Tour*. To Surtees it was truly democratic. At full gallop in driving rain all were equal, irrespective of their wealth or occupation: 'men in red, men in brown, men in livery, a farmer or two in fustian, all mingled together.'

The names of the masters of Dorset's hunts were better known than that of their MP. Almost their equal was the huntsman, who enjoyed his own status and social standing. One Piddletrenthide farmer thought a Dorset without foxhunting would make 'England unfit to live in', and he was not alone in such views. Throughout the season the weekly *Dorset County Chronicle* reported on the activities of the hunt and the number of foxes killed, just as the *Dorset Echo* now carries the football results.

The character of hunting in Dorset was shaped by its farming. The enclosure of the open fields supplied the hedges and double ditches and banks of the Blackmore Vale country. The great sheep runs of the downland were of open unfenced pasture, perfect scent-carrying turf. Purbeck and the south-east was largely heath. The agricultural depression indirectly helped hunting by reducing the amount of heavy ploughland.

For the first half of the 19th century Dorset was hunted at his own expense by one man, Henry Farquharson, of Langton Long near Blandford, whose fifty year reign extended the length of the county. During the 20 years from 1837 to 1857 he accounted for 3,312 foxes. After his retirement the hunting map gradually took its present form, with four hunts – the Cattistock, Portman, South Dorset, and Blackmore Vale.

At first, Dorset's landowners bankrolled hunting – building kennels, paying wages, improving the blood lines of their hounds. *Punch* called the 2nd Lord Portman 'Old Master'. Known initially as Lord Portman's Hounds and with kennels at Bryanston, his pack was regarded of as one of the best in the country.

When Thomas Guest, of the iron and steel family, retired as master of the Blackmore Vale in 1900 after hunting six days a week for thirty years a record field of over 1,000, most of them farmers, turned out for his final meet. Five years earlier, at a March meet, the fox ran through the open door of a cottage, swiftly followed by 17 couple of hounds, to the bewilderment of an old lady sitting down to her supper.

By the end of the century Subscription Hunts predominated, their members paying an annual fee. Hunting took place five days a week, with the field open to all and their territory extended by the coming of the railway. The Cattistock hounds could be put aboard an early train at Maiden Newton and be on the scent of a fox near Yetminster an hour later. Subscriber members could do the same, catching a train from London and keeping their horses at livery in Dorset. But the railway and the risk of hounds getting on the track were symptoms of change – of barbed wire, of farmers less willling to accept the right of fox-hunters to trample their fields, but there were few dissenting voices accusing it of cruelty.

The huntsman had little time for shooting, wanting foxes to be left in peace until cubbing in the early autumn. Conversely, gamekeepers thought foxes vermin to be shot and the hunt a disturbance to their birds. Technical improvements to shotguns and cartridges, combined with the easy rearing of large numbers of pheasant, had transformed shooting as a field sport. Coverts were planted to shelter young birds, crops to make them fly. Many mourned what one writer called the 'arrival of artificial game.' No longer did the 'old-fashioned country squire enjoy a moderate day with his neighbours.' Instead, birds were driven by lines of beaters over the guns, each with a loader at his side. The Prince of Wales made the sport fashionable. The age of the Edwardian 'Big Shot' had arrived. Neighbouring landowners vied with one another to provide the best sport.

From November to February Dorset's country houses filled with weekend house parties whose principal purpose was to produce a good 'bag': at Crichel (Lord Alington), Canford (Lord Wimborne), Milton Abbey (Sir Everard Hambro), Melbury (the Earl of Ilchester), Charborough (the Erle-Drax family) and Ilsington (Colonel Brymer). Lulworth (the Welds) was known for its hare and partridge, Grange (the Bonds) for its woodcock, Brownsea Island (Van Raalte) for its wildfowl.

Above: BERE REGIS (which is where the kennels were – and remain). The kill at a meet of the South Dorset Hunt in 1907. A contemporary article in the *Badminton Magazine* described it as 'a yeoman farmer's hunt. Go out any day you choose, look at the muster – a few ladies, a few top hats and black coats, two or three in pink and the rest of the field hard-looking men with keen eyes and workmanlike get-ups mounted on wiry business-like horses; you see at once what they are, the sinews of England, the best fellows you ever met, hospitable, generous, hard riders straight in word and deed – the yeoman of England.' This card was posted to Canada, and described a day out with the Cattistock, beginning at Upwey and ending at Abbotsbury.

Below: EVERSHOT. A meet of the Cattistock Hunt outside the Acorn Inn in about 1910.

Above: GRIMSTONE. The Cattistock Hunt, with the railway bridge and Viaduct Cottage visible at the bottom of the track.

The Meet. Horton Heath.

Above: HORTON HEATH. A meet of the Portman Hunt on Horton Heath. The pack was formed in 1858 by the 1st Lord Portman of Bryanston House. It's most celebrated pre First World War meet was in 1890, when the hunt met at Gussage All Saints on a 'crisp day with thin mid-winter sunshine'. Once the fox broke cover, one of the fastest runs on record began, covering 16 miles in 72 minutes and ending over the county border in Rockbourne. Interestingly, as with the number of girls in this photograph, more ladies than men were in at the finish.

Left: LITTON CHENEY. The Cattistock Hunt at Lower Cross Trees in 1890, when Rev Milne was Master. The large elm tree on the left had gone by 1960. William Cornick was a Bridport jam manufacturer, and the only one in the county.

PORTESHAM. A meet of the Cattistock Hunt near Hardy's Monument before the First World War. The hunt was established at Cattistock Lodge in the mid-18th century and at the date of this photograph its master was a hunting parson, the Rev E. A. Milne of Chilfrome: 'a rare judge of horse and hound, popular with all classes . . . he is known as "the fox killer", a sobriquet he has well earned, for no man can

hunt a fox from find to kill better.' Although 181 foxes were killed in 171 days hunting over the 1906-1907 season many more eluded the hounds, including a fox found near Hardy's Monument that was lost near Poxwell, nine miles away. One of Milne's predecessors as master, Lord Guilford, died after being rolled on by his horse when out hunting at Corscombe (there is a memorial to him in Sydling St Nicholas church).

MILTON ABBAS. Three photographs taken during the four days spent by Edward VII at Milton Abbey in December 1909 as the guest of Sir Everard Hambro, of the banking family. The King was there to shoot over the estate's 12,500 acres, and 10,000 pheasants had been put down for the occasion. Electricity was specially installed in the abbey and 'thanks to a liberal and judiciously-directed expenditure, the Milton estate is in the pink of condition.' The *Dorset County Chronicle* omitted few details in its flattering coverage of the royal visit, describing each of the three days shooting:

'As on Tuesday, when a capital shoot was enjoyed over the coverts on the Delcombe beat, the Royal shooting party left the Abbey at 10.40. There were ten guns out again, namely, the King, Lord Granville, Lord Savile, Colonel Ponsonby, Colonel Streatfield, Captain Lang, Mr Cosmo Bonsor, Sir Everard Hambro, Mr Eric Hambro and Mr Angus Hambro. The weather was clear and sunny, the sport excellent, and the King expressed himself much pleased. Luncheon was served at a tent near Ruins Cottage, and afterwards the Royal Party were photographed.'

By the time the King finally left Milton Abbey 2,700 birds had fallen to the guns. The three photographs show the 'Royal Party', the keepers and loaders, and the beaters in their white smocks.

Interestingly, when still Prince of Wales and looking to buy a country estate with good shooting, Milton Abbey was Edward VII's second choice after Sandringham.

H.I.M. the Kaiser at CRICHEL

Crichel Keepers

MOOR CRICHEL. In December 1907 the German Kaiser, Wilhelm II (back row centre with a feather in his hat), motored over from Highcliffe Castle, where he was recovering from an illness, for a day's shooting at Crichel. The house party also included Queen Victoria's third son, the Duke of Connaught and his wife, a German princess and cousin of the Kaiser (whose own mother was a Victoria's eldest daughter). According to the *Dorset County Chronicle*, 'Lunch was partaken of in a tent near the head-keeper's cottage, and was attended by the whole of the house party, who were afterwards photographed with the Royal guests by Mr Pottle of Wimborne.'

The lower photograph is of the keepers, who were issued with a new suit of clothes for the occasion. Interestingly, the Kaiser anglicised his name to William when signing the Crichel House visitor's book. The following day he planted a Cedar of Lebanon at Kingston Lacy and visited Corfe Castle, both then owned by Ralph Bankes.

LANES AND ROADS

CERNE ABBAS. An undoubtedly posed photograph intended to suggest the car is moving.

IN 1901 THE 16,650 HORSES IN DORSET travelled roads that had evolved over centuries. Some, like the drove roads, cut a straight path so as to get livestock to market by as direct a route as possible. Others wriggled their way from village to village, followed the river valleys, or climbed the downs. Tracks and bridleways developed in step to changes in farming. Lanes linked communities as they had always done. The clay lands of the Marshwood Vale had their holloways, Purbeck its chalk white ribbons through the heather. The first major change was the formation of turnpike trusts from the mid-18th century onwards. What are now Dorset's principal A roads all began life as turnpikes, either by straightening and widening existing routes, or by cutting new ones – creating a total of about 500 miles on which tolls had to be paid for their use.

In *A Country Childhood*, Henry Joyce's memoir of White Mill at Shapwick, where he was born in 1883, he described traffic as 'mostly slow and comfortable. One neither dawdled or hurried; but travelled at the pace of one's beast and enjoyed the scenery through which one passed.'

Traffic primarily meant the carrier's cart. Ralph Wightman gives a wonderful description of Piddletrenthide's carrier in *Take Life Easy*.

'Another free man was the carrier, Harry Hawker, who went the eight miles to Dorchester every weekday except Thursday. He left home at 8 a.m. and arrived at Dorchester at 10.30 a.m., returning at 4 p.m. unless there was someone expected on the 4.30 train. He got back at 6.30 to 8 p.m. It must be realised that a reasonably active man can walk eight miles in two hours, and that a horse can trot it in one hour, even over rolling hills. The carrier's horse seldom trotted and the able-bodied passengers were required to walk up the hills, but this did not account for two and a half hours on the road. This was made up by the endless stops in the first two miles of the journey through the straggle of houses along the valley. The carrier collected rabbits, eggs and butter for sale, and took orders for goods to be purchased in town. These ranged from groceries to unexpected lines, such as corsets.'

Carriers numbers slowly diminished as vans and lorries increased. So fearful of their threat to his livelihood was one carrier that he harnessed up his two mules and drove them down the middle of the road so that no car could pass. Dorset's last carrier was surely Johnie Canterbury of Stoke Abbott, who until his death in 1954 regularly drove his horse and cart to Bridport with commissions and Crewkerne to meet trains.

Also common were bicycles with solid tyres and the 20 cwt single horse van, popular with bakers, grocers and drapers (see page 55). At the back were two hinged glazed doors above a tailgate that doubled as a step. The front 30 inch wheels could be swivelled under the bodywork, allowing the van to turn in its own length.

The cost of maintaining roads was always vexed. Until the General Highways Act of 1835 rural roads were the responsibility of the parish and overseen by the local Justices of the Peace, an ad hoc arrangement that made many impassable in winter. The 1835 act granted parishes the right to levy a rate and appoint a salaried surveyor, whilst by the end of the century the cost of road maintenance was met by the newly-formed Dorset County Council. To maintain the road surface, flints were collected from the fields, mainly by women, stacked by the roadside, and then broken up, generally by old men with hammers who were paid by the yard – 'a slow and comfortable task for an old man on a sunny day,' thought Henry Joyce. In winter the pieces were spread on the roads, a little chalk added to bind them, then left for wheels to consolidate.

Thanks to the system pioneered by John McAdam (1756-1836), Dorset's major roads were composed of layers of small stones laid directly onto the subsoil, which were then consolidated and bound together by horsedrawn traffic. As long as there was adequate drainage, McAdam's invention worked well. But the sharp stones played havoc with the air-filled tyre of the motorcar: a 10 mile journey could easily mean three punctures. Amongst the earliest roads in Dorset to be sealed with tar-macadam were those in Bere Regis, where dust raised by sheep being driven to water in summer made the main street intolerable. By the 1920s the road-tarring gangs employed by the County Council were a familiar sight in the villages. Lanes dwindled into tracks. Tracks became footpaths.

Until the Motor Car Act of 1903/4 only steam-rollers and traction-engines of more than 3 tons needed to be registered. By law they were limited to four mph with a man waving a red flag walking ahead. Under the Act the registration letters 'BF' were initially issued to Dorset's motorcars, but following complaints the letters 'FX' were also assigned to the county. By 1914 the 1,200 cars listed in the records of the Dorset Motor Taxation and Licensing Department were trundling to and fro at the maximum permitted speed of 20 mph. In their wake came the first motorbikes, lorries and omnibuses, sowing the seeds of a revolution that has transformed the way we live our lives.

Above: ASHMORE. The carrier Isaac White (on the left) stands next to his son George in 1911 outside their small-holding at the bottom of Green Lane, once the principal track to Tarrant Gunville. This rural backwater on the southern side of the village was known as Well Bottom, and the covered well after which it was named can be seen behind the trap on the right. The cottage still stands. The vehicles under cover are typical carrier's carts, the ancestor of today's white van. in 1880 as many as 200,000 were still in regular use throughout England and Wales.

Below: BROADMAYNE. A corporal in the Dorset Regiment with his wife and children outside their Main Street cottage. In 1911 much of the village was put up for auction by its principal landowner, John Roberts Furmedge. The sale included 23 cottages, a brickyard, the village shop, and the Black Dog Inn, here seen on the left and still open today. Broadmayne bricks were famous. The last of its brickyards finally closed in 1939 when the lighting of fires at the kilns was forbidden because of the blackout regulations. The cottages on the left have been replaced by a short terrrace of modern houses.

Above: BURTON BRADSTOCK. Two cars parked outside the Anchor Hotel in about 1910. Note the uniformed chaffeurs and how the still rare motorcar has attracted the attention of the women watching from further up Barr Lane. In her book about Burton Bradstock, *Farmers, Fishermen and Flax Spinners*, Elizabeth Gale writes, 'The greatest excitement came when the new fangled motorcar travelled through the village. Driving through the main street was easy enough but the hills surrounding the village presented the early motorist with problems. The bigger boys would run beside the vehicles and then lend willing strength to push them when they conked out going up over Common Knapp or Mixen Gate Hill.'

Below: CANN. Looking down what is now the A350 towards Greyfriars Cottage and the old lane leading down to Cann Mill.

CHARMOUTH. Two views of the old Charmouth road to Lyme Regis. The road opened in 1825, crossing the upper part of the undercliff behind Black Ven, an area notorious for subsidence and cliff falls. Because it was also a wind funnel, it was known locally as Bellows Road, and with time and slippage became so precarious it was eventually abandoned. It closed to traffic on May 26 1924, to be replaced by the existing main road four years later. The upper photograph is of the Charmouth Cutting, the lower one a car passing Turnpike Cottage at Frost's Corner in 1910. The cottage was demolished at the end of the 1960s.

Below: DURWESTON. A Park's Removal Lorry from Portsmouth, balanced on the parapet of the bridge over the Stour at Durweston in 1925.

Above: EAST STOUR. A view looking east towards Fern Hill on what is now the A30 Shaftesbury/Sherborne road. The house on the left still stands, but the telegraph posts have all been removed.

Below: FONTMELL MAGNA. The Knapp in about 1910, with the Mill Street turning to Ashmore just out of view on the left. The barn and all the area beyond has since been developed with new housing. This is now the A350, whose only straight section are the two miles between Fontmell Magna and Sutton Waldron made when the new Blandford/Shaftesbury turnpike was opened. Until then, a winding lane climbed over the hill between the two villages.

Above: KING'S STAG. A line of cars outside the Green Man, chaffeurs at the wheel, in about 1906. FX 307 was a 60 hp Fiat belonging to Sir Randolf Baker of Ranston near Blandford and FX 387 was a 16 hp Vauxhall owned by Thomas Spiller of Luccombe Farm, Milton Abbas. LC4 is a London registration. Randolf Baker (1879 – 1953) was one of the pioneers of motoring in the county, and his predecessor to the Fiat, a 10 hp Panhard, was the second car in Dorset to be registered. Sir Randolf later became an MP for North Dorset. He also won two DSOs in the First World War whilst serving with the Dorset Yeomanry.

Below: KINSON. Few views in *Lost Dorset* are as unrecognisable as this one of the crossroads at Bear Cross, today one of the busiest roundabouts in the county. The Bear Cross Inn stood on the junction between the lanes to Wimborne and Longham. The card dates to about 1880, when the road from Bear Cross to Redhill was lined with small two acre farms. The inn was demolished in 1931, but if still open would be in the centre of the roundabout. Kinson has switched its allegiances more than any other parish in the county. In Dorset until 1931, it then became part of Hampshire, remaining there until the boundary changes of 1974, when it rejoined Dorset.

LONGHAM. Two views of the village. The upper one shows the River Stour and Mill Stream in about 1900. On the right is Bridge House, which later became an angler's hotel and tea rooms. The lower one is of a traction engine rounding the first bend after the bridge in 1920. The much enlarged Bridge Hotel now occupies the approximate area where the two cottages on the right once stood.

ZIG-ZAG, NEAR SHAFTESBURY

Above: MELBURY ABBAS. A treeless Zig Zag Hill in about 1890. The track from Shaftesbury to Tollard Royal via Cann Common originally connected to an ancient ox drove that ran along the top of the downs to Salisbury. It had 110 bends, but was long and steep: traces of its former route are still visible on the left when going down the hill. In 1837 it became part of a turnpike and the new route was cut, effectively making the hill a dual carriageway. At the bottom was a pub, a pond, and a now demolished toll-house.

Below: MELBURY ABBAS. Looking towards Dinah's Hollow and Shaftesbury from the track to Grove Farm House in 1906. The lane's high banks and unstable greensand mean that over time the surface has eroded. 'This is a view at the bottom of the hill just by our house. Doesn't it look nice?' wrote the writer of the card. It's not so 'nice' now, for the risk of a landslip caused its closure in 2014, leading to a much publicised campaign to find an alternative route and national headlines such as 'The silent way that was once a main road'. A section of bank did collapse in 2016, and although the road is now open again traffic is controlled by lights and reduced to a single lane by concrete barriers.

Left: MORECOMBLAKE. The still small hamlet sits astride the main Dorchester/Exeter road, though there is little sign of the traffic that now roars through it in this photograph of about 1900. On the right is the Sun Inn, on the left Sam Moore's bakery, with his bakery cart outside. The bakery started in 1880, and now, nearly 140 years later, remains the home of Moores Dorset knob biscuits. Moores is the only surviving bakery of Dorset knobs, hand-rolled and baked three times, which owe their name to their resemblance to Dorset knob buttons. A favourite biscuit of Thomas Hardy's, they have found a more recent role in the now biennial Dorset knob throwing competition, held on the first Sunday in May. The Sun Inn opened in 1823, closed in 1969, and is now a private house.

Centre: OSMINGTON. The card reads 'Autumn Sunlight in Osmington'. Just visible on the left is one of the earliest National Schools in Dorset, which opened in 1835 and is now a private house.

Left: PRESTON. The village in 1910. At the far of the lane on the right is the Ship Inn (now the Spiceship), whilst immediately behind the man sweeping the road is the post office. The buildings on the left have all been demolished.

STOURPAINE VILLAGE. NO. 2.

Above: STOURPAINE. The old and the new. A horse-drawn delivery cart and a parked car in a view looking north along Manor Road towards the junction with Havelins and South Holme in about 1910. The cottage on the left literally fell down and has since been replaced by a bungalow. Beyond the cottages on the right was the village school, with a reading room opposite – both now converted into private houses.

Below: STURMINSTER MARSHALL. A donkey cart passes the Round House in about 1890. The building no longer stands, but was built as a tollhouse on the 24 miles of new road belonging to the Puddletown and Wimborne Turnpike Trust (now the line of the A31). The turnpike's main promoter was J.S.W. Sawbridge Erle Drax, the owner of Charborough Park, who lost a considerable amount of money in laying out and constructing the new road. It was completed in 1840, seven years before the opening of the railway line from Wimborne to Dorchester via Wareham took away much of its purpose. Of the Round House, all that remains is its name, Roundhouse Roundabout, now the junction of the A31 and A350.

Round House, Sturminster Marshall.

Above: WINTERBORNE MONKTON. What is now the main Dorchester/Weymouth road (A354), looking north towards Dorchester. The building on the road was the toll-house, built in the 1840s and finally demolished in September 1965. The founding of the Weymouth, Melcombe Regis and Dorchester Turnpike Trust in 1760 improved the important route between the coast and Bristol and Bath. Bath was then the height of fashion, whilst Weymouth's heyday as the most fashionable watering-place in Britain lay ahead. The large house was the rectory and is now the Dorchester Learning Centre. The card is dated 1909, a year after the retirement of its rector for 42 years, the Rev William Miles Barnes, a son of the Dorset dialect poet.

Below: WINTERBOURNE ABBAS. The lane through the village in 1907. The building on the right with the tile roof was the Baptist Chapel of 1872, and next door was the post office. The view is little changed: only the almost constant traffic on the A35 is different.

Above: WINTERBORNE STICKLAND. A village outing in a fleet of charabancs, probably to Weymouth in the early 1920s. Two have easily visible Dorset registration numbers. FX6091 was an 'Old Rose' 20 seater 25 hp Selden belonging to Arthur Conyers of Blandford, seen on the right. On the left wearing a long white coat is the owner of the other charabancs, Lewis Sprackling, who ran Stickland Garage and also hired out cars and lorries. In the event of rain a large canvas roof could be pulled from the back. Unfortunately, the registration book including FX7359 has not survived, but it probably belonged to Sprackling.

Below: WINTERBORNE STICKLAND. A Fowler traction engine that turned over on Winterborne Hill in November 1904.

ENGINE ACCIDENT. STICKLAND HILL. NOV. 1904

Above: WINTERBORNE WHITECHURCH. Looking south up what is now the A354. The blacksmith's forge can be seen halfway up the hill on the right. Standing outside the Milton Arms are the thatcher Fred Hansford and Nat Cuff the village lengthsman, employed by the parish council to cut verges and keep drainage ditches clear between this and adjacent parishes.

Left: WINTERBORNE WHITECHURCH. The gateway on the right in the brick and flint wall was known in Dorset dialect as a 'drong', or a gate leading to a narrow passageway – in this case between some cottages and outhouses. All the thatched cottages on Blandford Hill were demolished for road widening on what is now the busy A354, one accidentally by a tank during the Second World War.

Below: WINTERBORNE WHITECHURCH. Sam Skinner delivering around the village for Ernest Foster, the village carrier. In summer he carried ice wrapped in sacking and straw from Blandford Station to the Ice House at Whatcombe, a mile up the valley. Sam joined the Dorset Regiment and died in action in 1918, six weeks before the end of the First World War. He is buried in Cerisy Gailley cemetery on the Somme.

ON THE HUSTINGS
POLITICS & POWER

THE ELECTORS OF TOLLER FRATRUM.

In Commemoration of the Return of COLONEL R. WILLIAMS FOR WEST DORSET, 14th May, 1895, by the large majority of 1213 Votes.

TOLLER FRATRUM. The electors of the tiny hamlet celebrating the return of Colonel Robert Williams as the Conservative MP for West Dorset after the 1895 May by-election, with the large majority of 1,213 votes. Unusually, his only opponent was George Homer standing on behalf of Independent Farmers with the support of the local Liberal party. The principal aim of the short-lived Independent Farmers Party was land reform as a way of breaking the domination of rural Dorset by a 'feudal aristocracy.' All 30 inhabitants of Toller Fratrum were tenants of Lord Wynford, so were well aware of which side their political bread was best buttered.

Between 1884 and the end of the century the political map of Dorset was completely redrawn. Prior to 1884 only those living in towns and owning or renting property worth £10 a year had the vote, leaving rural England without a political voice. Under Gladstone, the Liberals argued for 'one man, one vote'. Any reform was opposed by the Tories. Most agricultural labourers were employed by Tory landowners, who feared that once granted the franchise the working man would vote Liberal. But the 3rd Reform Act was passed, extending the vote to every male householder in the country, leaving only women still excluded. 1884 also marked the creation of elected parish councils for all rural parishes whose population exceeded 300 (those with less grouped together to meet the criteria).

The following year, 1885, Parliamentary seats were redistributed and their boundaries redrawn. Out went the old three member county division and eight boroughs – Poole, Weymouth, Shaftesbury etc. In came four divisions named after the points of the compass. Each covered approximately a quarter of the county, with about 8,000 registered votes, and returning one MP to Parliament.

Despite the 1885 Act the influence of Dorset's great landowning families remained undimmed. West Dorset's first MP was Henry Farquharson, owner of the Eastbury Estate at Tarrant Gunville. As well as representing neighbouring constituencies, Edwin Portman (North Dorset) and Pascoe Glyn (East Dorset) were the sons of neighbouring peers. Only South Dorset's first MP, the American-born Henry Sturgis, had no links with the county, but instead came from a wealthy banking dynasty.

By all accounts campaigning in the 1885 election was tumultuous and bad tempered. 'I hope that all bitterness, wrath, anger, clamour and evil-speaking will be put away,' wrote the vicar of Stoke Abbott once the ballot boxes had been emptied. The agent for the Conservative candidate in South Dorset, Colonel Hambro, went round Purbeck's clay-digging and heath-cropping communities offering to buy their bric-a-brac at an inflated price on the unspoken understanding that the purchase price included their vote.

All the candidates toured the county, speaking in village halls and school rooms in hope of attracting support. The *Dorset County Chronicle* nailed its political colours firmly to the mast, declaring that Colonel Hambro, 'whose election by a handsome majority is, we are sincerely glad to hear, as certain as any unaccomplished event can be.'

On election day polling stations remained open

until eight in the evening, allowing the farm labourer to complete his day's work and still have time to cast a vote. The provision of allotments was a key issue, and the Liberals 'Three Acres and a Cow' slogan helped sweep them to power in all but one of Dorset's four constituencies (West Dorset has only had Conservative MPs since its creation: Colonel Hambro lost South Dorset by 33 votes).

Four years later Dorset County Council was created. Until 1889 the county was run by unelected magistrates through the quarter sessions, using ratepayer's money for such things as maintaining roads and paying the police. Within a few years the County Council's responsibilities extended to sewerage and education, including school medical services. Once again, the political influence of

Dorset's landowners was in evidence. Of the 76 elected members in 1889 47 were peers, their sons, or what might be broadly termed the gentry.

In 1908 Asquith's Liberal government introduced Old Age Pensions, with the first weekly payment of five shillings for those over seventy being paid in post offices on January 1st 1909. Although it did not lead to the closing of Dorset's dozen workhouses the provision of pensions was a hesitant first step at welfare reform.

PUDDLETOWN. Electioneering in The Square during the January 1910 General Election. It was a fiercely contested election, forced on the Liberal Party Prime Minister Herbert Asquith by his failure to get the budget passed by parliament. The South Dorset seat was won by the Conservative, Angus Hambro, of the Milton Abbey banking family, who retained the seat until 1922, and later served as MP for North Dorset between 1937-1945. The 1910 Election ended in a hung parliament, leading to a second election later in the year, in which Asquith and the Liberals increased their majority.

WINTERBORNE STICKLAND. Electioneering in the early 20th century. The village is in the North Dorset constituency and Arthur Wills, a barrister and the Liberal candidate, won the seat from the Conservatives in the 1905 election, retaining it in 1906 and losing it – by a margin of 49 votes – to the Conservative Sir Randolf Baker in 1910. Note the poster on the right, a reference to the House of Lords being able to block legislation approved by the Commons: 'Are you content to allow the country to remain a peer-ridden nation?'

COUNTRY CRAFTS

WINTERBORNE WHITECHURCH. Thatching in the centre of the village in about 1910. The thatcher is John Davis. The cottage was known as Rats Castle because of the vermin, and was finally demolished in the 1940s. On the left, between the Reading Room and Post Office/Telegraph Office/Temperance Hotel, is the bakery with Bert Snook the baker.

THERE IS NO BETTER PROOF of the importance of the country craftsman than in the first and last villages listed in *Kellys Directory* for 1895: Abbotsbury and Yetminster. Between them they could muster four blacksmiths, four wheelwrights, three basketmakers, three boot and shoemakers, two saddlers, two millers, as well as a carpenter, thatcher and tailor.

Until the coming of the railways and the importing of factory-made agricultural machinery and mass-produced goods, rural Dorset was largely self-sufficient, its independence reliant on its craftsmen and women, on skills passed down from one generation to the next. Even a carpenter's nails were forged at the local smithy.

Some crafts were regional. Cranborne Chase and the east Winterbourne villages provided hurdlemakers, charcoal burners and flint knappers. Abbotsbury's trio of basketmakers owed their livelihood to the reed beds on the Fleet. Marnhull's limestone found work for masons, as did Purbeck and Portland. It was rare not to find a woman braiding nets in her cottage doorway in the villages round Bridport, or a country potter bent over his wheel on the clay beds near Verwood. Bere Regis, Broadmayne and the Lytchett villages had brickworks. The watermeadows on the Frome and Piddle their drowners, skilled in manipulating a network of hatches to flood the meadows and provide an early bite of grass for the stock. The orchards in the Marshwood Vale provided seasonal work for cidermakers. Dorset's village breweries rang to the cooper's hammer. Rushes from the Stour were woven into beehives, or trimmed into wicks for candles. A dozen or so villages had watchmakers, Bourton and Hawkchurch shoe-thread makers. There were lace and buttonmakers, glovers and tanners; chimney sweeps, carpenters, waggon builders, cabinet makers; makers of baskets, besom brushes, ladders, and hay rakes.

The sixty or so Bloxworth villagers directly involved in farming were supported by two blacksmiths and two carpenters. The carpenter's day might be spent hanging a gate, the next making a coffin. If the carpenter gave a cottage its windows and doors, it was the thatcher who kept out the rain. Dorset had one of the highest percentage of thatch roofs in the country, most of them using combed wheat reed. But it wasn't just cottages that depended on the thatcher. After harvesting and prior to threshing, ricks were built with sheaves of corn and then thatched, often ornamented on their tops with a cockerel. Once the corn was dry and ready for threshing, the thatch was removed and recycled for use on straw ricks.

In 1900 Dorset had about 3,000 boot and shoemakers. A labourers' hobnailed boots were a prized possession, costing a week's wages and usually replaced after harvest. To save money, the bootmaker in Worth Matravers, James Lowe, made 'straights', boots which could fit either foot. In *Under the Greenwood Tree* Mr Penny is first met sitting in his shop window, a boot on his knees, awl in hand, with rows of lasts, 'small and large, stout and slender', covering the wall behind him. Outside, the only indication of his trade, the upper leather of a Wellington boot was 'usually hung, pegged to a board as if to dry.'

Of all of the country craftsmen, the blacksmith was king. In 1901 there were 136,732 blacksmiths in England and Wales, of whom about 2,500 were in Dorset. As long as England remained horse-powered the blacksmith, wheelwright and saddler were sure of a wage. But the blacksmith did more than keep horses well-shod. He (and it always was a 'he') made scythe blades, billhooks, sickles, axes and pitchforks. One man might be left-handed, another need a long-handled spade. A woman might ask for a pot to be mended, a farmer his harrow or plough repaired. Some were journeymen, walking from one outlying farm to another doing odd jobs as they went.

Again and again accounts of rural life at the turn of the 20th century evoke the dimly-lit heat of the village forge, usually with a gaggle of ragamuffin boys peering in through the gloom. Now they are private houses, only their names recalling the original purpose: 'The Smithy', 'The Old Forge'.

Above: BISHOP'S CAUNDLE. The sign over the door at this group of cottages opposite the church combines two different professions. In 1895, Herbert Knott was the saddler and William Hutchings the postmaster (the post office door is behind the low wall to the left of the children), and both cottages are now a private house called 'Saddlers Cottage'.

Below: BOURTON. Edward Hindley established his stationary steam engine works in the early 1870s: one made in 1876 for the Gillingham Pottery, Brick & Tile Co can be seen running at the Sherborne Steam and Waterwheel Centre. By 1914 it employed 200 people (most of them men), making steam lorries, pumps, dynamos and saw benches, all of which were widely exported. The first casualty of the First World War was its waterwheel, thought to be the second largest in Britain, which was broken up and turned into ammunition. Local women replaced the men and the premises became a munitions factory, making parts for torpedoes and three million Mills bombs (hand grenades).

The woman half hidden at the very back of the top row under the Union Jack was Evelyn Clack, whose husband was killed at Arras nine weeks before the end of the war, leaving three children fatherless. The works closed in 1930, and the long derelict mill and foundry buildings have been demolished and replaced by housing.

Opposite page top: CHIDEOCK. The blacksmith John Burton (on the right) and his son Eli (on the left) outside their forge in the 1880s. Mrs Burton is standing in the doorway. The boy holding the pet rabbit, Robert Hussey, was the son of the village carpenter and wheelwright, William Hussey, whose shop stood nearby.

Opposite page bottom: KING'S STAG. A travelling knife grinder outside the Green Man. Every area in the county had its knife grinders, like Lovey and Joey Stanley of Wool, who moved from barn to barn as they plied their trade: Lovey boasted that she been born under an apple tree and never slept in a bed.

Above: BUCKHORN WESTON. The village forge in 1906. A new house occupies the site, though the one in the background still stands.

Below: CERNE ABBAS. Glove House, originally the site of a water-powered corn mill, later the Glove Inn, and later still a private house called 'Holly Bank', which tragically (and inexplicably) was demolished when Reginald Broadhead bought the Up Cerne estate in 1964. He also demolished Tucking Mill and some cottages before selling the estate 15 years later. The name stems from the leather glove and gaiter industry for which Cerne was once known. As an inn it was the first encountered by travellers entering the village from the north.

LYTCHETT MINSTER. A group of button workers outside South Lytchett Manor (now Lytchett Minster School) in about 1905. Button making in Dorset dates back to the early 17th century, when Abraham Case set up a cottage industry making 'High Top' buttons from a disc of sheep's horn covered in worked linen. By the early 19th century 4,000 women (and their daughters as young as eight) in the east of the county were making a whole range of buttons, which were taken to local depots for payment and collection. It was grinding intricate work and poorly paid, but the money saved many families from near starvation. The invention of button-making machinery in the Midlands proved a death blow, leading to widespread poverty and emigration. Thanks to Lady Florence Lees (seated front left) the industry enjoyed a brief revival in South Lytchett, and a button shop was opened to sell the buttons made by local outworkers under the auspices of the Lytchett Mission. Trade steadily diminished. In 1912 £38 worth were sold at a cost of £36, recalled the Mission's matron, 'Granny Speake' (seated front right). Three years later the button shop closed its doors, and after many years as an antique shop called the Old Button Shop it today stands empty.

MELPLASH. Thomas Cozens outside his carriage and wagon building yard in 1895. Thomas died in 1913 and is buried in the village. The business had been founded by John Trevett of Netherbury, a carpenter and wheelwright, whose son Robert, 'by strict attention to the business and carrying it on in temperance principles' (to quote from his memoir), expanded it to include waggon building and steam machinery, with ten employees. But there was a price to be paid. 'My father, being a most energetic and highly-strung nervous man, overworked himself and broke down with a severe attack of "Monomania",' wrote his son Isaac, who sold the business to

Thomas Cozens in 1892.

A carrier's cart is on the right and a Dorset wagon the left. Dorset wagons were of two types, a panel-sided bow-shaped wagon once found on the chalk downland, and the more common box wagon – such as in the photograph. They were usually painted yellow or blue, with red undersides. Note the elaborately decorated boarded tailboard giving the name of the builder and his address. Because Dorset wagons were low and wide, and easily manageable on a hill, their popularity spread throughout much of central southern England.

MILTON ABBAS. The smithy shortly after the First World War, when W. H. Evans was blacksmith: J. North is on the left. The village's much photographed two rows of thatched cottages were built by Lord Milton at the end of the 18th century. The smithy adjoined one of them, finally closing when Mr Evans retired in 1955 and is now incorporated in a private house.

THE SMITHY, MILTON ABBAS.

Lower St, Okeford Fitzpaine.

Opposite page top: NOTTINGTON. The octagonal house at Nottington began life as 19th century spa. It opened in 1830, its eight sides supposedly providing rooms for its builder, Thomas Shore, and his seven sons. Its sulphurous waters could either be drunk, or enjoyed as hot or cold baths, 'away from the hectic rush of modern living'. As Weymouth's popularity as a fashionable seaside resort gradually declined so also did that of the spa, and when this photograph was taken it was being run by a Mrs Frampton as a laundry. It is now a private house.

Opposite page bottom: OKEFORD FITZPAINE. Thatching in Lower Street on the road to Fifehead Neville, with the Royal Oak just visible on the left. The buildings on the right have been replaced, but the house being thatched still stands – though it was once condemned by the Council and only a local campaign saved it from being pulled down. The reed was probably local, for the harvesting of reed for thatching was once common along the Stour valley, whilst the spars used for pegging it down will have come from either hazel or willow.

Above: PORTESHAM. The village blacksmith and wheelwright, James Stickland, shoeing a horse outside his Front Street smithy, with Trafalgar Farm in the background. Under the horses can be seen the bonding platform, where wheels to be hot-bonded were placed with their hub in the central hollow. The protecting metal bar that wrapped round the outside of the wheel was measured and cut, the two ends welded together, then heated until it expanded sufficiently to slip over the wheel. Once hammered on, it was doused with cold water, which shrunk the metal and prevented the wheel catching alight. The platform was removed when work was being done at the neighbouring Half Moon Inn in the 1950s. Both smithy and inn are now private houses.

Above: SIXPENNY HANDLEY. Hurdle making in the woods. Thanks to the need to fold sheep over the downs, hurdles have long played an important role in Dorset's rural economy, specially on Cranborne Chase. The woodland was coppiced in rotation every seven years or so, as hazel's ability to regenerate guarantees a continuous crop. A true Dorset hurdle is made by weaving split hazel rods in and out of ten vertical stakes known as 'sails'. A small hole was woven into the middle, so that several hurdles could be threaded onto a pole and carried on a shepherd's shoulder.

Below: WEST MILTON. The parish register for 1862 records the marriage of Hannah Guppy, aged 25, to Thomas Knight, two years her junior. Both were higglers, as was Hannah's father Absalom. A higgler was a rural pedlar, selling anything from saucepans to patent medicines. They often took part payment in eggs or poultry, which then they sold on. Hannah used to sell her produce in Weymouth market, 'starting her journey almost in the middle of the night.' Thomas Hardy described them 'as an interesting and better informed class than agricultural labourers.'

ALONG THE COAST

BURTON BRADSTOCK. Gathering seaweed for use as a fertiliser on Hive Beach in about 1890.

DORSET has no truly coastal villages, as do Cornwall or Devon with their creeks and estuaries. The only natural harbours are those of Poole and Weymouth. From Charmouth in the west to Studland in the east, all the villages are set back slightly from the sea – earning their living from it, yet not wholly dependent on it. Portland's history includes much that is maritime, but because its villages are so closely interwoven with one another we have decided to bundle them together and place the entire Royal Manor in what we intend to be a second volume on the towns.

Once the railway reached Weymouth (1857) and Swanage (1885) the holidaymakers who crowded into them during the summer provided so profitable a market for the county's photographers they rarely ventured further afield. How could Charmouth's fossil-strewn beach compete with the arc of sand sheltered by the Cobb at Lyme Regis? The exceptions were Studland, Lulworth Cove and, to a lesser extent – and then only thanks to the railway reaching it in 1884, West Bay. Bournemouth's growth made Studland fashionable – indeed, it remains so still. Lulworth Cove's natural beauty brought paddle-steamers, whose passengers bought souvenir postcards to be written and posted once safely ashore.

"ALL ALIVE." MACKEREL. BURTON BRADSTOCK.

BURTON BRADSTOCK. 'All Alive'. Mackerel being landed on the beach. The fishing season was heralded by a look out on Cliff Road spotting the first shoal, usually in late April. 'When the fish are seen,' wrote Miss M. M. Crick excitedly in the *Victoria County History* of 1908, 'the look out signals or shouts, and at once the men run down pell-mell to the beach, their heavy boots thundering and their coats flapping as they run. The nets are snatched up from the beach where they are drying; the boats are hastily launched, and the school is pursued.'

Before the advent of feathers and spinners, the mackerel were seine netted. One end of the net was rowed round in a semi-circle, the other held by the 'shore-arm' team. The two teams then approached each other on the beach, hauling in the net and its catch as they did so. Just occasionally as many as 20,000 fish were landed in a single day. The money earned was divided into shares: two for the boat, two for the net, and one for each of the crew.

Above: BURTON BRADSTOCK. The ceremony of Blessing the Boats shortly after the First World War. They used to say of Burton that every man in the village was 'born with salt in his veins', and fishing once played a central role in its economy. Herring and sprats were salted down for the winter. Mackerel were sold, soused in vinegar, or eaten fresh. The ceremony took place on the old May Day, May 13, beginning with children walking round the village with garlands and the singing of traditional songs.

Below: EAST FLEET. The woman in the foreground is possibly Miss Fisher, who lived in one of the Butter Street cottages in the photograph and was mistress of the tiny village school, attended in 1895 by 23 children. The village is exposed to south-westerly gales and in the Great Gale of 23 November 1824 the church and five cottages were destroyed when mountainous seas swept over Chesil Beach. Many years later in 1897, at about the same date as this photograph, the only man living who had witnessed the storm, described how as a boy he had run for his life when he saw 'the tidal wave, driven by a hurricane, and bearing on its crest a whole haystack . . .'

EYPE. An Edwardian beach scene in the summer of 1913, with Golden Cap beyond.

EYPE. A torpedo from the Whitehead's Torpedo Works at Wyke Regis washed ashore in 1910. The company was founded by Robert Whitehead, an engineer who in 1866 invented a way of propelling a torpedo using compressed air. With the help of the Admiralty a site for the works was found at Wyke Regis on the shore of Portland Harbour, opening in 1891, and two ranges were established – leading to a succession of accidents (one hit a Norwegian freighter in 1904). Ironically, Whiteheads' torpedos played a significant role in both world wars, yet one of his granddaughters married a Bismarck and another the Austrian submariner Captain Georg von Trapp, whose children were immortalised in *The Sound of Music*. The Torpedo Works were demolished in 1988 to make way for housing.

Above: KIMMERIDGE. Clavel Tower served as a coastguard look-out between the wars, until becoming roofless and derelict and in danger of falling victim to the gradual erosion of the cliff. It was built in 1831 by John Richards, the owner of nearby Smedmore House, probably as an observatory and seamark. In 2006, the Landmark Trust, with a local charity and funding from the National Lottery, painstakingly dismantled the tower, labelled each of its 16,000 stones, and moved it 25 yards inland, where it was rebuilt as holiday accommodation.

Below: KIMMERIDGE. The Coastguard Station in about 1914. Note the Dorset gate on the left. Kimmeridge Bay and the ledges either side have long been a graveyard for shipping, made worse by the currents that sweep into the Bay. The Station opened in about 1820, and was originally commanded by a Naval lieutenant. Until 1896 there was also a lifeboat station at Kimmeridge, whose first oar-powered boat was the *Mary Heape*, launched in 1872 and which first saw service when a Norwegian full-rigged ship was driven ashore in a south-westerly gale. The Coastguard Station has been converted into cottages, and a weather-eye is now kept on the shipping off Dorset's coast by teams of Voluntary Coastguard Rescue Officers.

Below: OSMINGTON. The Regatta shortly before the First World War.

Left: LULWORTH COVE. The Cove's popularity was well-established in Victorian times, due mainly to the summer paddle-steamer services that plied between Bournemouth and Weymouth, stopping to offload their passengers for a walk ashore. On the left is the aptly-named *Victoria*, launched in 1884, requisitioned for service in both world wars, and finally scrapped in 1953. On the right is the *Majestic*, launched in 1901 and lost whilst minesweeping early in the First World War.

Below: RINGSTEAD BAY. Fishermen with their nets in about 1900, with the clifftop Coastguard Station on White Nothe just visible in the background.

Above: ST ALDHELM'S HEAD. A group of coastguards giving the tiny medieval chapel on the headland a spring clean. The Coastguard Lookout and adjoining cottages were built in 1895. Since 1994 the Lookout has been leased for 'one crab per annum if demanded' to the volunteers of The National Coastwatch Institution. The origins of the Norman chapel remain unclear, but one legend ascribes its construction to a local squire whose newly-wed daughter drowned in the notorious tide race off the Head. He afterwards built the Chapel as a chantry where a chaplain could pray for the drowned and whose roof could support a warning beacon.

Below: STUDLAND. The coastguard cabin on the beach in about 1890.

Above: STUDLAND. Fern Glen Refreshment Room on the Middle Beach, photographed in about 1905 when Studland first became fashionable. It was at about this time that Henrietta Bankes, the widow of Walter Bankes, of Kingston Lacy, released land for development, leading to the building of new housing on the road leading out of the village; 'a red brick epidemic' was how Frederick Treves described it. Amongst those who spent their summers there were various artists, including members of the Bloomsbury Group, and the philosopher Bertrand Russell.

THE LANDING STAGE, STUDLAND.

STUDLAND. Holidaymakers walking ashore along the precarious looking landing stage. Although the photograph was taken in about 1910, this card was written and posted on August 5th 1914, a week after the outbreak of the First World War. 'Having a wonderful time,' wrote its sender, 'though the war news takes the glint off everything.'

A visit to Studland by boat was an essential component of a Bournemouth holiday before the War, traps and carriages taking the visitors to Corfe Castle, Swanage, and other local beauty spots. The cottage in the background is Beach Cottage, which for many years was a café. Treves caught Studland's Edwardian flavour: 'A crowd of char-a-bancs and wagonettes will crowd its lanes in the summer, . . . while an ample refreshment room permits the tourist to have tea "at separate tables" on the beach.'

TYNEHAM. The Coastguard Station at Worbarrow Bay in about 1900. Note the chicken houses on the right. The line of black-painted single storey cottages stood below Hill Cottage and were here photographed from Worbarrow Tout. There were seven coastguards, who together with their families formed half the tiny fishing hamlet's population of 50. The Station closed in 1912 and was demolished on the instructions of Tyneham's squire, William Bond, who was afraid they might be converted to some other use. Today a stone memorial plinth marks the site.

WEST BAY. 'The Catch of the Season' aboard the *Silver Sprat*, though in this case the catch is mackerel. Traditionally, the mackerel season ran from March to midsummer, dominating life in the coastal villages once the first shoals were sighted. A Report into Dorset Agriculture describes one boat crew downing three hogsheads of cider while waiting for the tell-tale dark patch of ripples that marked the arrival of a shoal: 'The payment of this makes a great hole in the money earned when the fish do come.'

THE GENTRY

CHIDEOCK. Humphrey and Elinor Weld surrounded by their domestic staff outside
the entrance to Chideock Manor after returning from their honeymoon in 1908.
The AA was founded in 1905, and 'LA' was the prefix to a London registration
number. The Welds are Dorset's leading Catholic family and their principal estate is at
Lulworth. Thomas Weld bought the Chideock Estate, including much of the village, for
Humphrey's grandfather and successive generations of the family played an important
role in Chideock life until the manor house was finally sold in 1997.

In the summer of 1851 the 7th Earl of Shaftesbury (1801-1885) paid a first visit to his Dorset inheritance since the death of his father. St Giles House formed the sprawling hub of an 18,000 acre estate that included Wimborne St Giles and six other villages, as well as numerous farmhouses, a brickworks and pottery. You might think his response would be delight at so substantial a windfall. Yet here is his diary entry for August 22nd: 'St Giles's. Inspected a few cottages – filthy, close, indecent, unwholesome. But what can I do? I am half pauperised: the debts are endless; no money is payable for a whole year, and I am not a young man. Every sixpence I expend – and spend I must on many things – *is borrowed*!'

And borrow he did, building cottages, eventually opening three new schools and paying the salaries of their masters and mistresses. He encouraged allotments, evening classes for young men, laid out an estate cricket ground, and initiated an annual audit dinner for the tenants in St Giles House. Although the 'Good Earl's' championship of so many other causes made his Dorset visits rare, the estate prospered during the twenty or so golden years for agriculture that followed. When the tenants helped the pull the carriage of his grandson, the 9th Earl, and young bride up the drive to St Giles House in 1899 they were greeted by an indoor staff of 32.

St Giles was by no means the largest of Dorset's great estates – that honour belonged to the archaeologist General Augustus Pitt-Rivers (1827-1900) at Rushmore, whose 25,000 acres stretched in sizeable pockets the length of the county, from Farnham to Burton Bradstock. Virtually the entire Isle of Purbeck was the property of five men; Walter Bankes, Nathaniel Bond, John Calcraft, the Earl of Eldon, and Humphrey Weld, whose Lulworth estate was 15,478 acres.

These figures underline the power and authority wielded by Dorset rural landowners in the late 19th century. 'The great landlords of England are really the rulers of principalities,' wrote the *Fortnightly Review* in the 1880s. The worst were absentee-landlords, as in Hardy's Flintcombe Ash, 'a village uncared for by itself or by its lord.' The best did much to improve the living conditions of these in their care. In the east, Charlotte Guest and her daughter-in-law Lady Wimborne built over 100 cottages and three schools. In the north, at Motcombe, Grosvenor money paid for cottages and a school. Puddletown acquired four rows of terraced cottages. Throughout the county estate owners provided reading rooms, almshouses and recreation grounds. Their wives visited the sick, dispensed school prizes, subscribed to clothing clubs. Much of the church restoration that took place in the Victorian period was paid for by the squire.

But however benevolent a landowner, the gulf between the rich and poor was immeasurable. The big house was often the principal local employer, not just for its army of teenage housemaids, but also the gardeners in its hothouses and walled kitchen garden, the woodmen who fed its fires. Like it or not, living in its shadow meant a doffing of caps, of accepting the architect Gilbert Scott's assertion that the landowner 'is the natural head of his parish – in which he should be looked up to as the bond of union between the classes.'

And it was another architect, Norman Shaw, who best expressed the self-confidence of the ruling class in the mansion he built for the 2nd Lord Portman in the final years of the 19th century. Bryanston was one of the last great country houses to be built in Britain. Its £200,000 bill was paid for with London rents. Flamboyant, opulent, deliberately sited to dominate the surrounding landscape, its heyday was brief. 'With it,' wrote Andrew Saint in his book on Norman Shaw, 'the Portmans joined the great club of European aristocracy, not knowing that its days were numbered.' Within 30 years of completion its contents had been sold and the house put on the market.

Of the flurry of legislation through this period the 1894 reforms to death duties were the most divisive. They did not bring about the immediate destruction of the landed interest, as many peers prophesied, and in any case falling rent tolls had made owning land less attractive. But the increase in taxes to fund the First World War marked a watershed. 'England is Changing Hands' cried *The Times* in 1920, stating that a quarter of the country had been put on the market in the preceding four years. Estates crippled by taxation, 'their sons perhaps lying in far away graves', were broken up and fell to the auctioneer's hammer.

Dorset was no exception. In 1919 alone Cann, Cerne Abbas, Compton Abbas, Fontmell Magna, Halstock, Holnest, Melbury Abbas, and Stourton Caundle were all sold, as well as substantial pockets of land elsewhere, marking a change in the patterns of ownership in Dorset's villages and countryside that could never be reversed, and continues to this day.

ABBOTSBURY CASTLE.

ABBOTSBURY, Abbotsbury Castle. The first 'castle' was built as a summer residence to the west of the village in 1765 for Elizabeth, 1st Countess of Ilchester, whose family estates included Abbotsbury. Succeeding generations developed the now famous tropical gardens nearby, using the Gothick-style building as an occasional dower house. In 1913 it was destroyed by fire. The replacement shown in the photograph was then built on the site, but the First World War slowed progress. The materials used for the foundations were of poor quality, and after being abandoned the house was finally demolished in 1935.

CRANBORNE. Gardeners laying turf at the Tregonwell Lodge in 1904. The house was built in 1730 by James Stillingfleet, steward to the 1st Earl of Salisbury, owner of Cranborne Manor. After Stillingfleet's death it was bought by Thomas Erle-Drax, heir to the Charborough estate, who added the two wings and turned the Lodge into a fashionable country house. In about 1800 it was bought by Lewis Tregonwell, one of the founders of Bournemouth, whose heirs finally sold it a century later to the 3rd Marquess of Salisbury, then the Prime Minister, as a late wedding present for his eldest son, James Gascoyne-Cecil. The Cecil family still own it today. It is currently a private members club and boutique hotel known as 10 Castle Street.

DUNTISH. Duntish Court, which some architectural historians now regard as having been 'destroyed, quite unnecessarily' when it was pulled down in 1965. The house on Castle Hill was built in 1764 to designs by Sir William Chambers for an obscure Dorset landowner called Fitzwalter Foy on a site overlooking the Blackmore Vale. In about 1880 it was bought by Thomas Holford, a Mancunian whose wealth stemmed from the northern railway boom of the mid-19th century. Holford added a pair of pavilions, one of which is just visible on the right, and embarked on various alterations. Eventually it was in such a poor state that one owner set fire to it in order to avoid keeping up the pretence that it could be maintained. A single-storey house now stands on the site. What does survive are the walled kitchen garden and remnants of the 18th century pleasure grounds, including a lake and grotto.

Above: LANGTON LONG. Langton House in about 1910. The mansion was built by the foxhunting squire James Farquharson (1784-1871) between 1827 and 1833 to designs by the architect Charles Cockerell, and at the date of the photograph, though still owned by the family, was let. The bulk of the 6,000 acre estate was sold in about 1930. The house was requisitioned in 1941 and handed over to the Americans two years later, becoming the headquarters of the 1st Division. It was here that the scene of the fiercest fighting on D-Day, the assault on Omaha Beach, was planned. After the war it was bought by a demoliton contractor and gutted of anything of value. Explosive charges were drilled into the great classical façade and the house collapsed into a pile of rubble.

Below Left: LANGTON LONG. Benjamin Forder, then the tenant of Langton House, outside the South Lodge in his blue Crossley Brothers 20 hp Open Tourer. According to the 1911 Census, Forder was a cement and brick manufacturer. The South Lodge with its line of Doric columns is the least altered of the three entrance lodges to Langton House to survive.

Below Right: MILTON ABBAS. Frederick Cuff was a gardener at Milton Abbey and in this 1909 photograph is shown with a steam-powered lawnmower manufactured by James Sumner of Leyland, 'The Leyland Steam Motor Company' 1895. It weighed about 1½ tons. Cuff and his mower may well have been responsible for the 'beautiful undulating lawns' that greeted Edward VII later in the year (see page 133).

THE WHITE FARM, CRICHEL

MOOR CRICHEL. In 1892 the owner of Crichel House, Lord Alington (1825-1904) married a second wife, Evelyn Henrietta Leigh (1858-1939). One outcome of this unlikely late marriage was the creation of the White Farm by Lord Alington as a gift to his much younger bride. Its buildings, the smocks worn by those who worked there, and all its livestock, 'from the huge prize bull to the rabbits, cats and guinea pigs, and even the poultry are all white'. Here a water buffalo takes centre stage in what proved a passing fashionable curiosity.

TURNWORTH. The seventeen-strong domestic staff lined up outside Turnworth House in about 1900. Photographs such as this are rare, even more unusual are the smiles and general sense of having fun – all of which says something about the relationship between the staff and their then employer, the wonderfully-named Colonel Uvedale Edward Parry Parry-Okeden. The late 18th century Gothick style house stood in its own valley west of Blandford. In 1942 it was sold by his grandson, and was demolished following a fire in 1945. A single storey house now occupies the site.

Above: WALDITCH. An unusual aerial view of The Hyde, near Bridport, probably taken shortly after the First World War. The house was built in the 1850s by Joseph Gundry, of the Bridport net and rope making family. The real tennis court in the foreground was added in the 1880s by his son, and has had many lives since being played on by the Prince of Wales when a guest of the Gundrys. It first became a roller-skating rink, then a garage when The Hyde was occupied by the Americans as a military hospital during the Second World, then a cowshed, before becoming derelict. In 1998, following the founding of the Bridport and West Dorset Sports Trust, it was completely restored and is now one of only 25 real tennis courts in the country. The house is a residential care home.

Below: WIMBORNE ST GILES. The Dorset and Hampshire Yeomanry at camp in May 1914 in the park at St Giles House, the home of the 9th Earl of Shaftesbury (1869-1961). Lord Shaftesbury was in command of the South-West Yeomanry brigade, who, like all yeomanry, were part time soldiers much of whose training took place at their annual camps. There were 1,000 men and officers in the park, all with their own horses. Two years later, in February 1916, the Queen's Own Dorset Yeomanry took part in one of the most notable cavalry charges of the First World War, and one of the last. Under heavy fire, against Senussi tribesmen armed with machine guns, they charged across 1,200 yards of open desert, suffering 30% losses but ending a tribal revolt against British rule in Egypt.

THE RAILWAY

WEST BAY. A branch line train arrives at the station in 1906. The station opened in 1884 as Bridport Harbour in response to an optimistic plan to develop West Bay as a holiday resort, hence the change of name. It closed to passenger traffic in 1930, remaining open for freight for a further 36 years, principally for delivering coal and exporting shingle from the beach. The station building has had various changes of fortune, becoming a house, a boat yard office, boarded up, and West Dorset District Council Information Centre. Today it is a café called the 'Station Kitchen'.

DORSET WAS NEVER WELL-SERVED by the railways. Apart from the stone trade on Purbeck and Portland it lacked minerals worth exploiting. There was no heavy industry, no major port. Even when 'railway mania' was at is height in the 1860s, a speculator with a keen eye for costs would have taken one glance at Dorset's cocktail of miniature landscapes, few of them flat, and looked elsewhere for a decent return on his investment. Dorset's importance to the railway companies lay in it being on the route to somewhere else – principally the West Country, Bristol and the Midlands.

The first line to open was the Southampton to Dorchester Railway via Wimborne and Wareham in 1847. Ten years later the Wilts, Somerset and Weymouth Railway provided a north/south route between Weymouth and Yeovil, whose rural halts included Cattistock's two timber platforms, of which no evidence now survives. In 1862 the much-loved Somerset and Dorset Railway brought Wimborne within an hour of Stalbridge and the Somerset border. Other branch lines followed: to Portland (1865), Swanage and Abbotsbury (1885), West Bay (1888), Portland to Easton (1902). The opening of the Lyme Regis to Axminster line in 1903 completed a county-wide jigsaw that rarely turned much of a profit and shed most of its pieces by the end of the 1960s.

By 1914 the county's railway network had almost reached its peak. Sixty rural stations and halts served just under 170 miles of track, bringing the humblest hamlet within reach of the outside world. Only the villages in the Marshwood and Blackmore Vales, and those on Cranborne Chase and the central chalk downland, were more than a morning's ride in a carrier's cart from the nearest station.

The first to benefit were the more enterprising farmers, for whom the railway opened up new markets for their livestock and produce. Trains were reliable and kept to a timetable. Cattle and sheep could be sent to market, fresh milk shipped to urban centres outside Dorset, their waggons returning with machinery, fertilisers and animal feed. The milk factory at Sturminster Marshall was deliberately sited alongside the railway. The high levels of manganese in Bere Regis watercress helped strengthen the bones in Black Country children.

The coming of the railways irrevocably changed the texture of rural Dorset. The old drove roads and tracks gradually lost their importance. Barbed wire and corrugated iron began to appear. In *The Hardy Country* (1904), C. G. Harper lamented the loss of thatch in Bere Regis in favour of Welsh slates and mass-produced tiles. Describing Iwerne Minster two years later, Frederick Treves noted that the 'low thatched cottages are gradually vanishing, to be replaced by bold houses of gaudy bricks and tiles.' The principal goods traffic was coal, bringing additional employment and making homes less dependent on faggots for cooking and heat.

The construction of the lines across Dorset required a substantial labour force. Track had to be laid, cuttings and tunnels dug. Embankments, bridges, station buildings, signal boxes all had to be built – and maintained. Once completed, a job with the railways, even as a porter, brought prestige and a regular wage. A station such as Maiden Newton had a staff of a dozen. The village station master was a leading figure in the community.

Many of the changes are less easy to pin down. As literacy improved and increasing amounts of mail were carried by train so families were able to stay in touch. Among the postcards in this book are ones sent to Canada and Gibralter. Shop shelves gradually became stocked with goods and provisions from all over the Empire. Tourists alighted at beauty spots such as Corfe Castle and Abbotsbury. The London trains regularly brought down the wealthy owners of Dorset's country houses and their guests, specially in the hunting and shooting seasons – again providing rural employment. The raw recruits taught musketry at the Lulworth and Bovington ranges after they opened in 1896 reached Purbeck by train, initiating a military occupation that continues to this day.

The railways were also a means of leaving the countryside for the towns, even emigrating. They offered an escape from domestic service and poorly-paid farm work. It was the women who were the first to leave. In *Bound to the Soil*, Barbara Kerr described how in every Dorset village 'eager girls with small corded trunks awaited the carrier's cart to take them on the first stage of their townward journey.' They were the magnet that persuaded the men to follow.

Above: ABBOTSBURY. The station master, staff and passengers on the single platform in the early 1900s. Abbotsbury marked the terminus of a short branch line from Upwey Junction which opened in 1885, with additional stations at Upwey, Coryates Halt and Portesham. The line closed in 1952 and the station buildings were demolished ten years later. A bungalow now stands on the site and a public footpath follows the line of the former track bed. Many of the stones from the station were used in building a wall, and the former goods shed still stands alongside the footpath.

Below: DAGGONS ROAD. The station opened in 1876 on the Salisbury and Dorset Junction Railway to serve the growing community round Alderholt. The station is named after a nearby farm, as the railway company thought that it might get muddled with Aldershot if called Alderholt. The photograph shows the station master's house, the booking office and ladies waiting room: unusually, there was no platform canopy. The line closed in 1964 and the station master's house is now 'The Old Station Cottage'.

Daggons Road Station.

SHILLINGSTONE. The station opened in 1863 on the Somerset and Dorset Railway and closed in 1966. On the left is the 'up' platform towards Sturminster Newton with the main station buildings, including the canopy supposedly built for Edward VII who as Prince of Wales used to shoot at Iwerne Minster House (now Clayesmore School), the home of George Glyn, Lord Wolverton, a banker and Liberal politician. Although the track has been lifted, the main station building is a miraculous survivor, and the only station of the Dorset Central Railway to still stand. Following years of work by the North Dorset Railway Trust, much of it by volunteers, the station buildings have been restored to their mid-1950s appearance, the signal box has been rebuilt, a level crossing installed, a new shelter based on the original built on the platform on the right, and there is now a shop and café. The postcard is dated September 4th 1904.

SPETISBURY. The station opened in 1860 and closed in 1956. This photograph must have been taken shortly after the doubling of the line in 1901, for it shows a group of workers on the track bed and the new booking office and signal box. The buildings have been demolished, but the platforms survive and the station site is being renovated by the Spetisbury Station Project in hope of opening a visitor centre and café.

Above: TOLLER FRATRUM. A view of the tiny West Dorset hamlet, showing the church, manor house and surrounding farm buildings. The wooden railway worker's hut sits alongside the Bridport Railway Company branch line that ran 9½ miles from Maiden Newton to Bridport (extending to West Bay in 1884). The line opened in 1857, finally closing in 1975. Its only intermediate stations were Toller (Toller Porcorum) and Powerstock. In 1901, a few years after this photograph was taken, the Company was bought by the GWR. Eleven trains a day used the line. As well as coal, much of the goods traffic was cordage from the Bridport rope and net works, as well as milk and fish. With the outbreak of war in 1914 vast quantities of timber were felled in Powerstock Forest, which were then loaded directly onto the waggons. Bridport's factories provided hemp lanyards, rifle pull-throughs, hay nets for horses (50,000 a week at one point), camouflage and airship netting, anti-submarine cables – all of which would have been carried along the single track rural line.

Below: TOLLER PORCORUM. The station on the Bridport Railway opened in 1862, but this photograph dates to after 1904 when the platform was lengthened, and a station building and corrugated iron lamp room were built (just visible behind the train). The card also shows the loop in the line for a loading dock, principally for milk churns. The station closed in 1975 with the closure of the Bridport line, and the main station building was taken to Totnes as a terminus for the South Devon Railway. The platform largely remains, though covered in undergrowth. In the background is The Old Swan pub, now also closed and a private house.

FAIRS AND CELEBRATIONS

CANN. Children celebrating the Coronation of George V on 22 June 1911 outside the entrance to Cannfield Farm. The farm was part of the Glyn Estate, and like the lion's share of the banking family's 9,000 acres in Dorset was sold during a two day sale in Shaftesbury in 1919, when it was described as 'a residential holding of 164 acres with cowstalls for 35, stabling for 5 horses, pen and granary for calves, 3 pigsties and a fowl house.' The farmhouse stands at the end of a drive. Only one of the two greenstone lodges survive, and that stands derelict.

COUNTRY FOLK IN LATE VICTORIAN Dorset welcomed any excuse for a celebration. Every village had its summer fair or fête. There were the calendar customs, those linked to a specific date, festival or place. In East Lulworth, the imminent birth of a first child was announced by a woman known as the 'running gossip', who invited the village women to gather outside the expectant mother's door. As soon as the first cry of the baby was heard, a barrel was broached and the new father toasted. In Corfe Castle the members of the Ancient Order of Purbeck Marblers and Stone Cutters paraded through the village on February 14. Those hoping to join, the 'free boys', were entitled to kiss any woman they met during the parade. On Shrove Tuesday they were officially made freemen in return for money, a penny loaf and a quart of beer, after which the Marblers kicked a football round the village. In the Piddle Valley on Shrove Tuesday the children went from cottage to cottage singing their 'Shroving Song' in return for cheese or a pancake.

Haymaking, sheep shearing and the end of harvest traditionally meant a feast and dancing – as did May Day. About 20 villages had maypoles, of which Shillingstone's was the highest at 118 feet. In Wool the village sweep danced with the May Queen. Elsewhere children carried garlands from house to house, later linking hands round the maypole and dancing the 'Dorset Ring Dance' to a village band. Along the coast, the garlands were loaded onto boats and thrown into the sea to bring luck for the mackerel season ahead.

Another regular excuse for a celebration was the annual Club Walk by the members of the Friendly Societies. They existed in most Dorset's villages of any size and were described by William Barnes as 'the finest fortresses against the inroads of want and misery that man ever erected.' Prior to the advent of the welfare state the Friendly Societies acted as a rural safety net, their members paying regular contributions into a common fund in return for medicine and money when sick or old, and a decent burial when dead. Members had to be healthy when they joined and were mostly shopkeepers and craftsmen. Those receiving money were forbidden to visit a pub or leave their cottage between sunset and sunrise, whilst 'any member who marries a second wife knowing the first to be alive shall be obliged to quit the Society immediately.' They helped bind comunities together, providing convivial companionship. The annual feast day was the highlight of the year and attendance was compulsory.

Barnes wrote a wonderful account of a North Dorset Club Walk:

'First went a band of wind-instruments, and then the flag, on which were printed "the bee-hive" and "joined hands", with other emblems of industry and friendship; next to this were the honorary members . . . and lastly walked the Friends, two by two, and each bearing the badge of the Society, a knot of ribbon in his hat. The members were watched by the ruddy young women of the village, pointing out, or nodding to, their brothers and friends in the procession: and even the old women, who spent fifty summers of the year in squalid indolence by the glowing embers of the cottage hearth, took the staff that supported the almost forgotten form of her grandmother, and tottered to church.'

A Christmas highlight was the appearance of the mummers, a group of half-a-dozen or so men who toured the inns and big houses in return for beer and money. The play's principal characters were St George, a villain (usually a Saracen), a comic doctor and someone to collect the money at the end. In West Dorset there was often a hobby horse and a man dressed as Father Christmas's wife. In the east the costumes were covered with strips of rag or cloth. Much beer was drunk – so much so in Chetnole that on one occasion the mummers sang songs to a haystack which they mistook for a house.

Opposite page top: BERE REGIS. Driving sheep down West Street to the Woodbury Hill Fair in 1895. As well as a grocer, baker and corn dealer, Samuel Bemister sold ironmongery, books, seeds and patent medicines. The five September days of the Woodbury Hill Fair were once a highlight of the Dorset year, celebrated by Thomas Hardy as a thinly disguised 'Greenhill' in *Far From the Madding Crowd*, 'The busiest, merriest, noisiest day of the whole statute number.' By the date of this photograph its glory days as a major hiring and livestock fair were over. Reduced to two days, the first for the sale of livestock and provisions, the second was 'Pack and Penny Day', when everything was sold off cheaply so the stallholders did not have to reload their carts and carry away unsold goods.

Opposite page bottom: BURTON BRADSTOCK. The Floral Fete 1920, with Rookery Cottages on the right. The First World War had only ended 18 months earlier, hence the car disguised as an armoured car on the left. The green two-seater Ford belonged to Colonel William Forbes Panton, who served throughout the war, initially with the Dorset Regiment in Mesopotamia. The fête took place on July 22, beginning with a church service and a procession through the village led by the Bridport Artillery Band, followed by lunch in the schoolroom. There was a baby show, country and maypole dancing, as well as horse-jumping, a display of decorated waggons and a fancy dress contest.

Right: CERNE ABBAS. The Townsend's roundabout at the 1909 village fair. Townsend's travelling fair, once familiar throughout Dorset during the summer season, was founded in 1876 by William Townsend, whose job on a mail coach fell victim to the expansion of the railway network. With nine mouths to feed, he bought a small children's roundabout which packed away in a horse-drawn cart: once set up, the horse then turned the roundabout. The family slowly prospered, eventually moving to Weymouth. William's seventh son, Richard, owned the ride in the photograph and built the swinging boats just visible on the right. The steam-driven roundabout was worked by a traction engine called *Empress of the South*, which was requisitioned in 1914. At the table near the roundabout the family sold paper confetti, which they laboriously cut by hand and sold for 1d a packet so people could throw it when riding the galloping horses. I am indebted to Kay Townsend, the great-granddaughter of the fair's founder, William, for her help with this photograph.

Below: CHETNOLE. The Mummers, Christmas 1911. The traditional Dorset mumming play involved St George fighting a Saracen or Turkish knight, but there were endless variations, both on the plot and characters involved, including the appearance of a hobby horse. Also included in this photograph are Father Christmas and his wife, who was always played by a man and who after being killed is brought back to life by a comic doctor. The mummers went round the village, performing in return for beer and small sums of money. The First World War brought mumming to a close, and the only surviving play in Dorset today is the one performed in Symondsbury, near Bridport.

CORYATES. The Sunday School Treat, July 1911. Coryates is no more than a few cottages near Portesham, though a school and a house for a mistress were built there in 1869. This photograph, which shows the adults sitting at a well-laden table and the children in lines on the grass, suggests that the 'treat' was less for the pupils than it was for their parents and those involved in running the school.

Above: CRANBORNE. To celebrate and mark the end of the First World War a national Bank Holiday called Peace Day was held on July 19 1919. The weather was appalling, and the event was only a partial success. In truth there was little to celebrate. The leader in the *Dorset County Chronicle* reflected the national mood. 'Now that the Peace Celebrations are over and the flags put away, most people will be glad to put all thoughts of war behind them and get rid of every reminder of the world's greatest tragedy.' Here a band and members of the local Oddfellows lead the procession.

Below: EVERSHOT. Celebrating the Coronation of George V on 22 June 1911. This was the last great imperial Coronation. 'In every scattered portion of the globe,' cried the official account of the day, 'where even a handful of British subjects was to be found, the day was celebrated in fitting fashion. From East to West, from far Cathay to distant Canada, the chain of celebration circled round the globe, and the flag floated out at noonday to the thunder of cannon and the strains of the National Anthem.' In Dorset rain rather dampened things.

Above: PUDDLETOWN. The annual outing of the Friendly Society. Puddletown Brass Band, well known throughout the county, leads the procession down the High Street.

Below: SIXPENNY HANDLEY. The annual fête in 1912. The village fête was organised by the Oddfellows Society. There were usually two bands, one of them the well-known Handley Silver Band, and there was the traditional procession of decorated carts and waggons to a nearby field, where as well as races (ponies, donkeys, children, adults) there was a steam roundabout, shooting galleries, swing boats, coconut shies and a cricket match on the Common. Writing in 1940, but recalling the turn of the century, F. Adams wrote: 'In August 1914 came news of war. All our old customs suddenly ceased. There were no more club walks or fetes. . . Our village life was entirely changed and there are not many of us left who can look back to those peaceful days . . .'

SHROTON. Shroton Fair shortly after the First World War. Shroton Fair was traditionally held near Michaelmas Day, on September 26 and 27th, and was one the main events in Dorset's rural calendar. For many years time was dated in this part of Dorset by the fair: Ralph Wightman writes of old men recalling events by the number of months that had passed before or after it and William Barnes celebrated it in 'Shrodon Fair', one of the most humorous of all his Dorset dialect poems. An old Dorset saying insisted blackberries should not be picked after Shroton Fair as the Devil had spat on them.

Originally a hiring fair, it gradually incorporated roundabouts, rides and other attractions – including one year a travelling menagerie complete with tiger. The fair eventually lost its importance, and though known as the Fair Field much of the site is now occupied by the cricket pitch.

Bartlett's Steam Fair was established by three brothers near Fordingbridge, and much like Townsends (see Cerne Abbas) began with a child's pony roundabout, which in 1872 was converted into a steam-driven set of galloping horses, adding an organ and renaming it 'Barlett's New Forest Hunters'. Tragically, the gallopers were destroyed by rival gangs of fans at the 1960 Beaulieu Jazz Festival, and the only survivor is in the Beaulieu Motor Museum.

SPETISBURY. Tourism comes to Dorset in the form of George and Leo Primavesi, of 35 Raeburn St, Brixton: seen here doing the washing-up 'On the Stour, near Spetisbury, Dorset. Sept 1906'.

Below: STOKE ABBOTT. A group photograph taken for the 1913 Club Walk. A first cousin of the Friendly and Oddfellows Societies, the village Club was once an institution throughout the county. Stoke Abbott Club was founded in 1870 by the rector William Austin-Gourlay and by 1900 had over 100 members. Those drawing sick pay from its funds were banned from pubs or allowed to leave their homes between sunset and sunrise. The Club Walk took place on the first Friday in June with much celebration, a feast, dancing and a surfeit of cider. Villagers decorated their houses with streamers and the members walked in procession behind the Beaminster Band, each of them carrying a wooden stave decorated with ribbons. The tradition continues, with a Walk playing a central role in the annual Stoke Abbott Street Fair in July.

TARRANT RUSHTON. On the back is written, 'Taken Feb. 14th 1905 – after a village wedding.' A decade or two earlier *Cornhill Magazine* imagined a farm labourer 'some fine morning, before he is two-and-twenty, on his way from church, with his bride, who is only seventeen.' In reality both bride and groom were likely to have been in their mid-twenties. Pregnancy before marriage was common and thought nothing of, though grandmothers continuing to have children were looked down on: 'when the young 'uns begin 'tis time for the old 'uns to finish.' The brick and flint Dellsmead cottages were built by the Crichel Estate and remain largely unchanged.

TOLPUDDLE. An alas poor quality postcard of the outing of the Friendly Society in 1907. Although the Tolpuddle society was formed in 1833 to support the wages of farm servants it called itself The Friendly Society of Agricultural Labourers. Its six founding members were led by George Loveless, a Methodist lay preacher, who intended it both as a mutual benefit society and as a vehicle for protesting against the gradual lowering of agricultural wages. In 1834 a local landowner and magistrate, James Frampton, wrote to the Home Secretary saying that its members had sworn a secret oath – and it is was that they were arrested for, not the forming of the Society. The six men – the Tolpuddle Martyrs – were tried in the Shire Court in Dorchester, found guilty, and sentenced to seven years penal transportation in Australia. Such was the outcry (there were marches, petitions) they were pardoned two years later. The Trades Union Movement hads been born. By 1907 Tolpuddle's annual outing had shed its political relevance in favour of a band and light-hearted procession.

UNIDENTIFIED POSTCARDS

We have been unable to identify the location of the five postcards that follow, and any help will be gratefully received (by email either to barrycuff.dorset@yahoo.co.uk or online@dovecotepress.com). The second photograph was taken by Worrall of Blandford, and the winter scene on the next page was sent to an address in Okeford Fitzpaine in 1909, apart from that we know nothing.

Acknowledgements

This book could never have been published without Barry Cuff's willingness to allow the use of his remarkable collection of Dorset postcards, surely the largest outside the Dorset County Museum. Again and again he has provided new acquisitions to help fill gaps. He knows as much as anyone I have ever met about many of the obscurer aspects of Dorset's history, and has written the captions for the villages in the east Winterborne Valley, where he spent his childhood. The photograph of Frederick Cuff on page 176 is of Barry's great-uncle. His friendship and enthusiasm for this project have been *Lost Dorset*'s greatest pleasure.

Our choice of illustrations has not been based on trying to include a postcard of every village in Dorset – apart from anything else there are some for which no postcard is thought to have been produced. It was never our intention to only select photographs of a place that is truly 'lost' – although many do. What we have tried to do is choose those that give a sense of the way of life in rural Dorset in the late 19th and early 20th centuries – a period of upheaval and change as great as any in its history.

At an early stage in researching the postcards I decided to try and track down the exact location of all 350 postcards so as to see what had changed and to avoid making unnecessary mistakes. If anyone wants their faith in human nature restored they should go out into Dorset's villages, as I have done over the last eighteen months, and wave an old postcard in front of complete strangers and ask for help in identifying where it was photographed. Without their encouragement, their willingness to join me in the hunt, often giving freely of their time, as well as inviting me into their homes and putting on the kettle, I would never have discovered as much as I have or found some of the views shown in the postcards. Remarkably, in some cases, they knew the names of the people in the photographs, despite their having been taken over a century ago.

I would like to thank all of them, many whose names I did not write down: they include Bridget and Dave Bowen, Rita Cruise O'Brien, Chris Bright, Peter Collis, Valerie Dicker, Angie and Mary Frizzle, Harold Gill, Judith Hewitt, S.E. James, Margaret Morgan-Grenville, Alan Riggs, Anna Stiles, George Taylor, John Tory, Kay Townsend, Bernard Trowbridge, Mary Wrixon, and Hattie Young.

The single biggest change since I wrote *Dorset Camera 1855-1914* in 1974 has been the invention of the internet. Many villages have created their own websites, often of a high quality and a great help. The same is true of family websites, again allowing me to breathe new life into some of the faces shown in the postcards. The Dorset Online Parish Clerks website, opcdorset.org, created and maintained by volunteers, has been invaluable. It lists every parish in the county, providing a brief history and transcribing records such as census returns, and should be a first port of call for anyone interested in Dorset's past. The National Library of Scotland website includes the Dorset Ordnance Survey six-inch to the mile maps from the late 19th century, allowing me to pinpoint a handful of buildings I might otherwise never have traced.

A considerable number of excellent village histories have been published since 1974, rarely if ever for much financial reward. Many include contributions from men and women whose memories reach back to the period covered by *Lost Dorset*. My debt to all of them is considerable.

I owe a special thank you to Sam Johnston and the staff of the Dorset History Centre for their help and suggestions in tracking down information, and for allowing the inclusion of the map of Dorset on page 7. Fingers more nimble than mine made the use of the History Centre's microfilm reader an easier task than it threatened to be.

The research for this book has taken me the length and breadth of the county. Rural Dorset has changed out of all recognition in the 150 years since the earliest postcards in this book, but it remains remarkably unspoilt. Of course, cottages have been demolished, shops closed, roads widened, and new housing built, but a child in a photograph of 1900 would find much that remains familiar today.

Yet the pressures facing rural Dorset are considerable, and a failure to stand up and shout when faced with planning decisions that ignore the county's character and architectural traditions could easily destroy much of what makes Dorset so special.

Further Reading

Allan, Vivienne (ed), *West Stafford Millennium Book* (2000)

Anderson Graham, P., *Iwerne Minster Before, During and After the Great War* (1923)

Bailey, C.J., *The Bride Valley* (1982)

Barnham, Diana, *The Gussages, Past & Present* (1994)

Barnes, Tim, *My Dorset Days* (1980)

Barnes, William, *William Barnes, The Dorset Poet* (ed C.J. Wrigley) (1984)

Barter, Charles H.S., *Melbury Osmond*

Bettey, J.H., *Man & The Land* (1996)

Betts, Robin, *Richard Brinsley Sheridan of Frampton* (2012)

Blad, Anthony, *Yonder Ground* (1993)

Bond, Lilian, *Tyneham, A Lost Heritage* (1956 &2012)

Bowen, Bridget & Dave, *Remembering Piddletrenthide* (2015)

Boswell, B., (ed) *Leigh, A Dorset Village* (1986?)

Breach, Bob, *Melbury Abbas* (1998)

Bright, Mervyn, *Buttony, The Dorset Heritage* (1971)

Brocklebank, Joan, *Affpuddle in the County of Dorset* (1968

Brown, Alan, *A Backward Glance at Wool* (undated)

Brunnen, J.G., *The History of Stour Provost* (1996)

Buchanan, Mary, *Compton Abbas* (1991)

Clark, Laurence, *Motcombe Miscellany* (2012)

Coffin, Leslie, *Dorset Villages (Past & Present)* (1984) *Cerne Abbas & Villages* (1987)

Coomer, Bill, *Bailey Gate, The Milk Factory 1888-1978* (2000)

Creed, Sylvia, *Dorset's Western Vale* (1987)

Cruise O'Brien, Rita, *Together, Life in a Dorset Village* (2014)

Draper, Jo & Copland Griffiths, Penny, *Around Verwood* (1999)

Eastwood, John, *The Chideock and Seatown Book* (undated)

Farley, Ron., Thorncombe (1995)

Fernandes, G.W.L., *Stourton Caundle* (1974)

Forty, George, *Dorset, The Army* (2011)

French, Godfrey, *Stoke Abbott, West Dorset* (1974)

Fuller, Margaret D., *West Country Friendly Societies* (1964)

Garrett, Eric, *Bradford Abbas* (1989)

Graham, Tom, *Fippeny Ockford and Thereabouts* (1954)

Gibbons, A.O., *Cerne Abbas* (1962)

Good, Ronald, The Old Roads of Dorset (1966)

Greenland, Robert, Bradford Peverell (2001)

Greenhalgh, Audrey & Guttridge, Roger, *Ferndown* (1999)

Haggard, Rider, *Rural England* (1903)

Hallett, Paul & Annette, Chetnole (2007)

Hann, Melvin, *Bobbies on the Beat* (2006)

Hardy, Thomas, *Personal Writings* (ed. Harold Orel) (1967) *Under the Greenwood Tree* (1872) *Far From the Madding Crowd* (1874) *Tess of the d'Urbervilles* (1891)

Harvey, O.D., *Puddletown* (1968)

Hill, Michael, *East Dorset Country Houses* (2013) *West Dorset Country Houses* (2013)

Hill, Shelagh (ed), *The Book of Yetminster* (2005)

Horn, Pamela, *The Real Lark Rise to Candleford* (1976)

Jones, Mary D., *Cerne Abbas* (1952)

Joyce, H.S., *A Country Childhood* (2000)

Kerr, Barbara, *Bound to the Soil* (1968)

King, June, *Memories of a Dorset Parish, Bygone Lytchett Minster* (undated)

Knott, Philip, *The Book of Stourton Caundle* (2001)

Langford, Marie, *Cattistock* (undated)

Lawrence, Ian, *Fontmell Magna in Retrospect* (1988)

Legg, Rodney, *Dorset Sporting Runs* (2001)

Lehane, Brendan, *Dorset's Best Churches* (2006)

Lemmey, Pam, *A History of Halstock* (1984)

Lindsay, Hugh, *Litton Cheney in the Bride Valley* (1993)

Marsh, Bernard, *Memories of Dewlish* (undated)

Medlycott, Mervyn, *Sandford Orcas* (2009)

Melbury Abbas WI, *A History of Melbury Abbas* (1985)

Mingay, G.E., The Victorian Countryside (2 vols) (1981)

Moore, Doris, *Footsteps from the Past, Bourton* (1968)

New, Roy, *I Remember, Village Life in Old Dorset* (1989)

No author given, *Story of Piddlehinton* (1990)

Norman, Andrew, *Corfe Remembered* (2017)

Oakley, Mike, *Dorset Stations, Then & Now* (2016)

Page, William (ed), Victora County Histories, *A History of Dorset* (vol II) (1908)

Percival, Shirley, *Lytchett Matravers* (1989)

Phillips, Sheila (ed) *Sydling St Nicholas* (1993)

Pride, Marjorie G. C., *Memories of Bockhampton and Bockhampton School* (approx 1984)

Pike, Muriel (ed), *The Piddle Valley Book of Country Life* (1980)

Pitfield, F.P., *The Book of Bere Regis* (1978)

Portesham Church School, *Under Black Down* (1968)

Portman, Marjorie, *Bryanston, picture of a family* (1987)

Rampisham WI, *A History of Rampisham* (1988)

Sandison, Annette, *Trent in Dorset* (1969)

Saville, R.J. *Worth Matravers* (1990)

Sherry, Desmond, *Dorset Crafts & Trades* (1974)

Shillingstone Parish Council, *Around the Maypole* (2000)

Stanier, Peter, *Dorset Mills* (2000)

St George, Kate M., (ed) Child Okeford (1999)

Taylor, Ann, *The Book of Spetisbury* (2006)

Taylor, Sue, *A Short History of Affpuddle, Pallington, Briantspuddle, Throop & Turnerspuddle* (undated)

Tennent, R.J., *A Purbeck Parish, Church Knowle* (1963)

Treves, Frederick, *Highways & Byways in Dorset* (1908)

Turing, Bruce (ed) *Sixpenny Handley, The Story of our Parish*

Vine, Richard, *Studland* (undated)

Viner, David, *Roads, Tracks & Turnpikes* (2007)

Wightman, Ralph, *Take Life Easy* (1969)

Wirdnam, Audrey, *Pidela* (undated)

Young, Jimmy, *Old Dorset Brewers* (undated)

Index